THE BOOK OF ELY

BY

PAMELA BLAKEMAN

BARON
MCMXCIV

Pamela Blakeman

FIRST PUBLISHED IN 1990 AND IN THIS REVISED IMPRESSION
IN 1994 BY BARON BIRCH FOR QUOTES LIMITED

PRODUCED BY KEY COMPOSITION, CHENEY & SONS,
HILLMAN PRINTERS (FROME) LIMITED AND WBC BOOKBINDERS

ISBN 0 86023 550 5

Contents

Acknowledgements

Whatever merit this book may have, much is due to the people of Ely; it is their book because it is about their past and present and many have helped me with it. Among them it is impossible to single out anyone apart from the late Reg Holmes, who encouraged and increased my interest in the City's past. Of others I particularly thank Dr Dorothy Owen, Diocesan Chapter Archivist, Elizabeth Gatland, who in the first instance urged me to write this book, and Clifford Manning, all of whom have read through the script and for whose advice and guidance I am most grateful. The staff of the Cambridgeshire Collection at the Cambridge Central Library, the Cambridgeshire County Record Office, the University Library and the Ely Library have been unfailingly helpful and I thank them all.

Key to Caption Credits

AAG	Aberdeen Art Gallery and Museums, Aberdeen City Arts Department.
BL	Brian Lane
CAS	Cambridge Antiquarian Society
CC	Cambridgeshire Collection, Central Library, Cambridge.
CCM	The Lord Bishop of Ely and the Church Commissioners for England.
CEN	*Cambridge Evening News*
CI	Courtauld Institute of Art
CCIS	Cambridgeshire Cottage Improvement Society Ltd
CW	Colin Wills
DC	Dean and Chapter, Ely Cathedral
DM	Donald Monk
ECDC	East Cambridgeshire District Council
EM	Ely Museum
ES	*Ely Standard*
ESC	The Ely Society
JH	John Hardiment
LG	Leslie Garner
MR	Mike Rouse
MT	Mallyon Thompson
MW	Mary Wills
PC	Governors of Thomas Parson's Charity
SAL	Society of Antiquaries of London
UL	University Library Cambridge
VA	By courtesy of the Board of Trustees of the Victoria and Albert Museum

THE BOOK OF ELY

FRONT COVER: This oil painting, c1857, looking down St Mary's Street towards the Cathedral, is by Henry Baines, son of a King's Lynn sailor; he trained in London. The Cromwell Arms is on the left and the small toll house on the right, next to the White Lion public house. The octagon and lantern are as restored by James Essex. (MT)

'Legend of St Etheldreda, Her Marriage. She parts from her husband. She builds her Abbey at Ely. Her Burial' These panels, framed together, hang in the meeting room of the Society of Antiquaries in London. Painted in distemper on a ground of gilt gesso in the 15th century, they were discovered by Canon James Bentham c1800 'acting as the doors of a cupboard in an Ely cottage . . .' (SAL)

Foreword

by The Rt Rev Peter Walker, Bishop of Ely (1977-1989)

I warmly commend this book by someone whose love for Ely is matched by an exceptional knowledge of the City and its great Cathedral, its past life and its present.

We live in days of turmoil. Such a book as this speaks of the continuities among change. These are the things that the great Cathedral – the 'Ship of the Fens' – stands to speak of as it rides the storms of history.

This well-researched book will give such a glimpse, with new things for those who love Ely already, and for those who come to this very special place for the first time..

December 1989.

Dedication

For Elizabeth

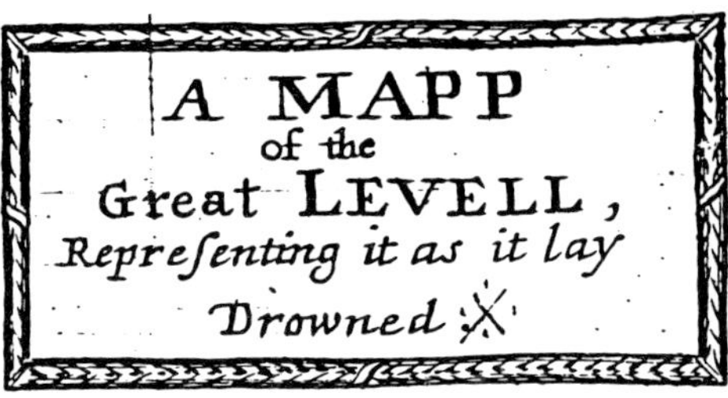

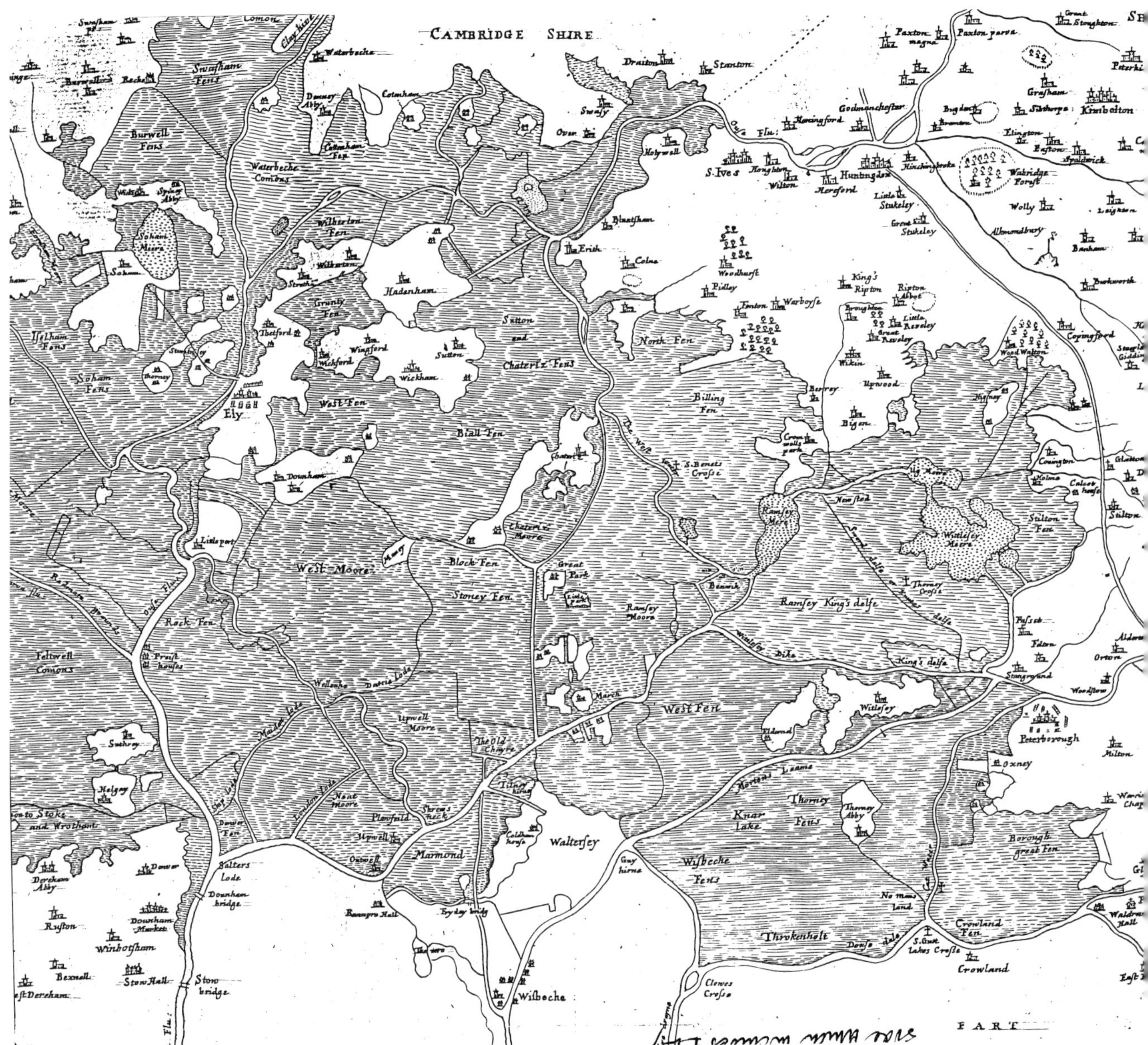

ABOVE: This map of the 'Great Level, Representing it as it lay Drowned' was first published in William Dugdale's *Hist of Imbanking and Drayning of Divers Fenns and Marshes* etc 1662. The map is oriented with the north to the bottom. OPPOSIT Etched by R. Farren c1880, this view has changed little, though a row of cottages were built (1892) in the centre and t trees on Babylon to the right are no longer there. Today the Cutter advertises Norwich Brewery.

Introduction

Ely is special: a small country market town with a magnificent cathedral. Because of its size and situation it differs in some ways from the other more prosperous and larger cathedral cities in East Anglia but it has a long and interesting history. So far as I have been able, I have tried to discover the truth, but that has been no easy task as there is rarely a concensus opinion about any past event. I hope that this book may be a starting point for more detailed and expert research into the various facets of Ely's history; I intend eventually to deposit a copy with references at the County Record Office.

The Tabula is a curious painting said to have been copied in Tudor days from an older picture. It shows 40 monks and 40 Norman knights with their coats of arms who, during the knights' stay at Ely, became close friends. When the Normans eventually left, it was with 'Howling fearful to be heard' from their friends. *(Reproduced by courtesy of The Lord Bishop of Ely and The Church Commissioners for England.)*

In the Beginning

The City of Ely, its title retained by Royal Warrant granted in 1974 by Queen Elizabeth II, is set on a low hill rising above the surrounding 'great level of the fens', with the River Ouse flowing at its foot. It was on this hill that St Etheldreda founded a monastic settlement in 673. The present Cathedral of the Holy and Undivided Trinity, a great architectural treasure and house of prayer, continues to dominate the City and to be a landmark for many miles as it has for more than 800 years. Grouped around, it is claimed, is the largest collection of mediaeval buildings still in daily use in this country. A see was established in 1109 by Henry I, which separated Ely from the enormous Diocese of Lincoln and the monastic church became the seat of a bishop and so properly styled 'cathedral'; it was dedicated at that time to St Peter and the Blessed Virgin Mary, later to St Peter and St Etheldreda.

The early history of the fenland area is one of continual change; flooded by freshwater, flooded by sea, linked with the land mass of Europe, frozen, perhaps wooded and covered with clay, silt and peat deposits. These changes took place over many thousands of years and affected different parts at different times. By the end of the Ice Age, higher land in Ely had a covering of Lower Greensand; later a few small areas received deposits of Boulder Clay. Ely, on the eastern side of a small 'fen island' extending about seven miles east-west, about two miles to the north of the City and about five to the south, is surrounded now, not by marsh and mere, but by 'stretches of rich black peat soil varying in depth from a few inches to several feet'. This black peat soil provides some of the flattest, richest and most intensively farmed land in the country, though its lightness can lead to spectacular 'fen blows' in dry spring weather. The fact that Ely is not surrounded by water is due to the drainage of the area begun by the Romans and continued intermittently until the 17th century. In 1630 the Bedford Level Corporation under, first the Earls and later, the Dukes of Bedford, assisted by Dutch engineer Cornelius Vermuyden, began a more systematic programme. As the water drained from the sponge-like peat into small channels the ground level sank and it gradually became necessary to pump water up into the larger channels, which were embanked as they were by then at a higher level than the surrounding country. Most of the waterways in the fens look like canals but are not called that, but rather dykes, drains, leams, eaus or rivers, depending on their size. Windmills, at first used to raise the water into the main drainage channels, were replaced with pumps powered by steam engines, then by diesel engines and more recently by electricity. So an artificial landscape, a definition that would perhaps surprise many natives of the fen area, has been created.

St Etheldreda was born, probably in 630, at Exning near Newmarket, one of the four daughters of East Anglian King Anna. She was married in 652 to Tondbert, probably the earliest known ruler of the island of Ely and a prince of the South Girvii, or Fenmen. Three years later, after his death, the *Anglo-Saxon Chronicle* tells us that she returned to Cratendune which, with the rest of her land, had been cared for by her steward, Ovin. This land, on the site of present day Bedwell Hay Farm, may have been given to her by Tondbert. It is said that Etheldreda, whose first marriage, at her wish, had never been consummated, was not left for long in peace; after four years she made a political marriage, this time to Egfrid, son of Oswy of Northumbria. The legend tells that Egfrid was only a boy half Etheldreda's age and he agreed she should continue her celibate life. He later changed his mind but Etheldreda evidently refused to comply as, guided by Wilfrid, Bishop of York, she went to Coldingham in 672 where her husband's aunt Ebba was Abbess. Soon Egfrid set out to fetch her back to his court but Ebba heard of his intention and advised Etheldreda to flee to the island of Ely. Legend has it that the runaway Queen would have been caught by Egfrid but a 'sudden inundation rendered the roads impassable'.

So Etheldreda returned home and at first she decided to found her monastery near the remains of the first church built on the island, close to the Roman Akeman Street. This building, almost destroyed by Penda earlier in the century, may have been sited at Cratendune. It was on slightly higher ground, just over 21 metres above sea level, on or near the site of the present Cathedral, that Etheldreda founded a monastery in 673. Here she was consecrated Abbess of Ely by her friend and adviser, Bishop Wilfrid. The monastery was intended for about 70 nuns and monks but in fact only 40 to 50, under a simple rule, lived there together 'loving the worship of God and preserving the beauty of the house of the Lord'.

About seven years later, on 23 June 679, Etheldreda died, evidently owing to some kind of tumour on her neck; in the presence of a 'sorrowful company' she was interred as she was said to have requested, in a plain wooden coffin. She was succeeded as Abbess by her sister Sexburgha who, some 16 years later, arranged for the first translation of Etheldreda's body, traditionally said to have taken place 17 October 695. Bede tells us that the monks searched for and found near Cambridge a coffin of white marble, which was brought by boat to Ely. When Etheldreda's coffin was opened 'a great miracle had occurred and . . . the body . . . was entirely free from corruption'. After this a variety of miracles were said to have taken place associated with the wooden coffin and with her grave clothes. Sexburgha was succeeded by her daughter, Erminilda, so the first three Ely abbesses were both queens and East Anglian saints.

As to what Ely was like and who the people there were in the early days of the monastery, the monastic builders would have used readily accessible materials such as mud, wood and reeds, though perhaps the church was partly of stone. The homes grouped around the monastery were simple buildings whose occupants either worked as servants at the monastery or helped to supply food and other necessities to the nuns and monks. During the summer months nearby fen land was used for grazing, while on higher ground fruit and vegetables were grown. Fish and birds were important sources of food, and ale the usual drink as no water was sufficiently pure.

Life in Ely was relatively peaceful for about 200 years until the 9th century Danish incursions disturbed eastern England. About 870, the Danes sacked and burnt the Abbey at Ely with those at Crowland and Peterborough, and Edmund, King of East Anglia was martyred. Most of the gold and silver treasures, illuminated manuscripts and vestments which the monastery must have owned, vanished from Ely. Although a small number of nuns and monks returned to the Abbey, it was not until c970, after a period of which little is known, that the monastery was re-founded as a Benedictine house; previously it was not apparently of any particular order. The new monastery was for men only and was housed in new buildings consecrated by Dunstan.

It is with King Edgar's charter of re-foundation that the probable origin of the mediaeval Liberty of the Isle of Ely, with its independent jurisdiction, whereby the Prior held his own court and received financial benefit, can be found. The King conferred rights of 'some sort' over the Isle of Ely, later to become known as a palatine state. This re-establishment was largely due to the fact that, under King Edgar, AEthelwold of Winchester 'formed a deliberate policy of restoring monasticism' in the area. His negotiations to ensure that the monastery was well endowed proved 'his tireless industry and remarkable competence . . .'.

In the years after 970 the Abbey continued to acquire land and, though it is difficult to build up a continuous picture of its expansion up to the Domesday Survey of 1086, there are some examples of this in the *Anglo-Saxon Chronicle* and the *Liber Eliensis* (the 10th century Book of Ely). Bishop AEthelwold 'bought many villages from the King and made it [the abbey] very rich'. Another example concerns land in eight villages given by three brothers when sons of two of them entered the monastery. In the 10th century a considerable amount of land from nearby East Anglian counties was given by Brihtnoth, Earl of Essex; this was followed with further gifts of land by his widow and, it is said, a tapestry curtain 'worked with the most memorable acts of her Husband's life'.

Brihtnoth was killed fighting against the Danes at Maldon in Essex 991. A memorial recording the date, but incorrectly calling him Duke of Northumberland, is in Bishop West's chapel in the Cathedral. The addition of Wisbech and part of Whittlesey soon followed so, by the early part of the 11th century, the Abbey at Ely held more land than at any other time.

Early in the 11th century, King Canute with Queen Emma visited the monks at Ely for the festival of the Purification of the Blessed Virgin Mary, often known as Candlemas. This is remembered now in a snatch of verse set to music by Dr Arthur Wills, cathedral organist, 1987.

'Merrily sung the monks of Ely
As Canute the king rowed by
Row nearer the land, knights,
And let us hear the monks sing.'

Perhaps it was on a visit to this festival in another year that the journey, never easy in winter, was found more difficult. The route, about six miles from Ely, crossed the frozen Soham mere and here one improbable story suggests that Canute said 'Hold ice or break ice, I will keep the feast of the Purification with the good monks of Ely'. A 'fenner' of 'exceeding fatness', nick-named Budde or Pudding, led the way to test the ice and so Ely was reached in safety.

Later, D.J. Stewart in his *On the Architectural History of Ely Cathedral* of 1868 tells us King Harold appointed as Abbot, Thurstan, 'a Fenman, born at Witchford, near Ely, who had been brought up in the monastery, and had acquired the rare accomplishment of reading Latin as well as English'. After the Normans conquered most of the country, Thurstan was joined by the Earls of Chester and Northumberland and by the young Hereward. It was probably under Hereward's leadership that the Isle of Ely proved the last stronghold to hold out against the Normans. He destroyed each new causeway begun by the Normans almost as soon as it was started; spells cast over the Saxons by a witch proved unsuccessful and attempts to hire Fenmen only led to Norman soldiers being killed. It was not until the way into Ely, either along the causeway from Stuntney or along the one from Aldreth, was betrayed to the Normans (probably by the monks) that Hereward was forced to yield c1071. However, he has become a figure of legend so it is difficult to know what truth there is in his story.

By the time of the Domesday Survey of 1086 Simeon, a kinsman of King William, had been appointed Abbot at Ely. The survey is inconsistent and much is omitted so it is not possible to assess the population, existence of a market or of a castle. What is clear is that eels in their thousands were caught nearby (24,000 annually at Stuntney), that there was a vineyard at Ely and that there was meadow and pasture land. There were villagers who owned some land, cottagers who probably did not and also a number of serfs. The land which belonged to the

Abbot of Ely, in common with that in many other places, declined in value soon after the Conquest but regained value by 1086. The Ely Abbey still had many holdings throughout East Anglia as well as in Cambridgeshire; some close to Ely as at Little Thetford, Witchford, Wentworth and Witcham, others further north at Doddington and Wisbech. The *Liber Eliensis* lists many precious items of church plate, rich vestments and other treasures held by the monastery towards the end of the 11th century. By the 13th century the church at Ely also held the two hundreds of the Isle of Ely, which stretched up beyond Wisbech, the five and a half hundreds of Wicklow in Suffolk and one and a half hundreds near East Dereham. The Bishop and the Prior also had many manors in East Anglia.

ABOVE: A distant view drawn and etched by R. Farren in 1880, gives some idea of the approaches to Ely, certainly in the winter, before the fens were drained. BELOW: The silver gilt mace of the Bedford Level Corporation. (V&A)

LEFT: St Etheldreda carved on a fine stone boss in the Cathedral presbytery. (DC) RIGHT: During the journey from Coldingham to Ely, Etheldreda and her companions fell asleep and when they awoke her 'walking-staff had taken root in the ground and was become a pliant sapling, with fresh bark and budding'. This is one of the eight carvings on the octagon columns which tell the story of her life. CENTRE: Private individuals were not allowed to own swans; this was one of the marks of ownership used by the Bishop of Ely in 1581, cut or branded on the upper surface of the bird's beak. In 1766 the Bishop appointed an officer to govern his rights of 'Hunting, Hawking, Fowling, Fishing, Swanning and Shooting . . .' BELOW: A second carving, reproduced from Bentham's history, shows the first translation of St Etheldreda; when the tomb was opened 'no trace was left of the disease under which she had died, and a small scar on her neck was the only mark'.

ABOVE: Engraved by Samuel and Nathaniel Buck in 1743, this view of Ely is surprisingly unchanged.

BELOW: The funeral of Richard Cox, thirty-fourth Bishop of Ely from 1559-1581: this large oil painting (six and a half feet wide) hangs in the Bishop's house. It is in two sections; the left hand side, apparently painted in reverse, shows a gallery which links the Bishop's Palace to the Cathedral and the right shows the scene in the choir where a bishop delivers the sermon. *(Reproduced by courtesy of The Lord Bishop of Ely and The Church Commissioners for England.)*

LEFT: The coat of arms with the motto 'Arridet Aridum' which may be translated as 'The dryness is pleasing' or 'Dry land pleases' in a stained glass window at Bedford House, Ely. BELOW: 'Old Overfall Mill, Ely; Robert Cross in Boat. His Ancestors lived here about 150 years ago,' c1910. The mill and bridge were on a corner along Queen Adelaide Way, shown on the 1885 map as Middle Fen Bank. RIGHT: Men at work to improve a main pumping drain in Middle Fen before mechanisation. (CC) BELOW: Tradition has the headless body of Bryhtnoth, Earl of Essex rowed back to Ely by the monks for burial in 991. This panel is part of a stained glass window in St Mary's Church. (BL)

Building for God

When Abbott Simeon came to Ely in 1081 he was an old man of over 80, said by some authorities to be in his 87th year. Simeon must have been a vigorous and determined man as by 1083 a new building on a grand scale had been started. Why was it necessary? Perhaps the existing building was in poor condition or perhaps it was considered too humble to express the glory of God, and doubtless a new building would have been a great symbol of Norman power. Work was begun east of the present choir with the foundation of an apsidal east end and continued westward until Simeon's death in 1093, by which time the oldest parts of the present Cathedral, the transepts, had probably been started. During the next 100 years a central tower, the nave and a western tower about 50 metres high with, to either side, a western transept of great beauty, were built. There the architecture gradually changed from the round-arched Norman or Romanesque to the pointed Early English style. Cloisters extended southwards; two magnificently carved doorways, known today as those of the Prior and the Monks, led into the nave from the west and east walks and a third doorway into the south transept. These doorways, though two are now partly hidden, demonstrate the great skill of the craftsmen of the twelfth century and also the Continental and Scandinavian influences. Although building may not have progressed at a regular pace the Norman church was completed by 1189. The greater part of the stone in the Cathedral was brought to Ely by water, chiefly from the quarry at Barnack north of Peterborough, but also from quarries in Lincolnshire, Caen in France, Purbeck in Dorset and elsewhere.

Changes in the status of the monastery took place, although the Prior continued to be its head, when Henry I suppressed the office of Abbot in 1109. Hervey, the last Abbot, became the first Bishop. 'He declined, both for himself and his successors, all liability to maintain the fabric, and threw the whole charge on the monks . . .' but obtained exemption from the payment of tolls for the transport of materials needed for the repair or construction of the Cathedral. Property belonging to the monastery was divided between Bishop and monks. Ely, unlike other cathedrals, still has no bishop's throne though, previously used by the Abbot and Prior respectively, today both Bishop and Dean each have a canopied stall at the western end of the choir.

When in 1539 the monastery was dissolved by Henry VIII, Bishop Goodrich retained his position and stayed in it beyond the new Foundation of 1541. The charter established the 'King's New College at Ely' which consisted of 'a Dean, 8 canons, ''eight peti-canons, four students in divinity, xxiiii scholars to be taught grammar, six aged men decayed in the King's wars or service'' also staff to manage the estates, and singing men and boys'. It was then that the dedication was changed from St Peter and St Etheldreda to that of the Holy and Undivided Trinity.

Much of the Norman building remains today, though there have been changes, one of the most noticeable the loss of the north-west transept. This was apparently in a ruinous state when

Daniel King made a drawing in 1650, and later an engraving of the view from the north. Dr Dorothy Owen, Diocesan and Chapter Archivist, says that it was *this* transept that collapsed after the storm of 1700 and that architect 'Grumbold was employed to build the large buttress'. In many parts of the building traces of colour are still evident, reminding us that the interior was once painted red, green, blue and gold, though later covered over. There is now a clear view of the whole length from east to west, no longer interrupted by the Norman pulpitum. This had stretched across the nave between a pair of columns to the west of the crossing and was apparently demolished, either when the choir was moved eastwards in about 1770, or about 30 years later.

Many of the capitular buildings date from the Norman period too, including the monastic infirmary, as can clearly be seen from the columns, capitals and arches in what is now known as Firmary Lane near the south door of the Cathedral. The present roadway was roofed and was the main hall of the infirmary. On the north side is Powcher's Hall, on the south the Black Hostelry, named from its earlier use as a place in which visiting Benedictine monks received hospitality; today visitors can find 'bed and breakfast' accommodation there. After the Reformation these buildings formed houses for the Cathedral clergy. At the east end of the lane, part of the infirmary chapel can be seen, incorporated into a building used for many years as the home of residentiary canons, later as the Deanery and from 1986 as the Chapter House of the Dean and Chapter. The mediaeval Chapter House, the monks' dormitory and the former St Catherine's Chapel had been situated near the south entrance, but were demolished in the mid-seventeenth century. Other work of the Norman period includes the range of servants' quarters along the street known as The Gallery, the undercrofts of the Almonry and the Priory and part of the mainly 18th century house known as the Canonry.

The earliest addition to the Norman church was the porch at the west end, built in the early 13th century in the Early English style with, for the first time at Ely, stone vaulting. This was a two-storey building, considerably altered during the 19th century, when the great doors were refaced with wood and new decorative ironwork added. This includes small birds – martlets – which appear in the coat of arms of the Waddington family who financed the work. Today it is known as the Galilee porch, though there is some doubt as to exactly which part of the west end originally had this name or why it was so called. Perhaps it was used in Sunday processions, which 'symbolised Christ going before the disciples into Galilee'.

Bishop Northwold, largely at his own expense, then built in the same style the six-bay presbytery at the east end, to accommodate the increasing number of pilgrims to St Etheldreda's shrine, and to provide a more suitable setting. Here the Early English style can be seen to advantage in the tall, narrow lancet windows, columns with detached shafts of Purbeck marble, deeply undercut stiff-leaved capitals and stone vaulting with carved and painted bosses. This presbytery was dedicated in September 1252 in the presence of Henry III and his son, Edward. The changes necessitated the demolition of most of Abbot Simeon's east end; the only remaining traces are the two tall columns, one on either side, at the east end of the present choir. Changes were made toward the end of the 14th century to allow more light to fall on Etheldreda's shrine. Today no certain remains of that shrine exist, but the position is marked by a marble slab with the words 'HERE STOOD THE SHRINE OF ETHELDREDA SAINT AND QUEEN WHO FOUNDED THIS HOUSE A D 673'.

Building continued with the large and spacious Lady Chapel; begun in 1321 it is placed, not at the east end as is most usual in England, but at the eastern corner of the north transept. Carved in clunch, a local hard chalk, are elaborate hooded ogee arches, between which are sculpted scenes based on the life and legends of the Virgin. Traditionally, money for this project was discovered when a foundation trench was dug and a workman 'struck his spade upon a brazen pot full of old coins, buried in the earth'. It was completed soon after John of Wisbech, the man responsible for much of the work there, died from the Black Death in 1349. It must then have been rich and jewel-like, with much stained glass and painted decoration.

The year after building started on the Lady Chapel the peace of the main structure was disturbed by a not entirely unexpected event. On 12 February 1322 the central Norman tower collapsed towards the east with a crash, so as 'to make the whole city to tremble and to cause men to think that an earthquake had taken place'. The monastery was fortunate; in Alan of Walsingham it had a sacrist of vision and imagination who, though first dismayed by the catastrophe, soon used the opportunity to create 'one of the greatest surviving miracles of the middle ages'. Under his direction, with the assistance of expert craftsmen, including William Hurley, later the King's carpenter, the central space was widened to form an octagon, with sides of two different lengths. Eight great columns were constructed to support the stone octagon and above it the lantern tower of wood covered with lead; the two rise to a height of about 45m. The three bays of the present choir, damaged when the tower fell, were rebuilt and roofed with a stone lierne vault. The vaulting of the lantern is of painted wood with a central life-size carving of Christ in Glory. The octagon and lantern took about 20 years to complete and cost over £2,000. In the days when bells were rung 'the wood thereof shaketh and gapeth, (no defect but perfection of structure) and exactly chocketh onto the joints again . . .'. Whether or not this is true, the structure has certainly survived, although subject to change and restoration.

In addition the monks built a new church c1362 for parishioners who, when they worshipped at the nave altar of St Cross, interrupted monastic services. This was a lean-to church alongside the north nave aisle of the Cathedral and, when it fell into ruin, the parish was moved into the Lady Chapel and became known as Holy Trinity. It was only in 1938, when this parish was finally united with that of St Mary to form the Parish of Ely, that the Lady Chapel was returned to the care of the Dean and Chapter. The 50th anniversary of the union of the two parishes was celebrated at a special service in the Lady Chapel on Easter Day in 1988.

The survival of the central octagon is a miracle but the octagon, with the four corner turrets placed on the west tower at the end of the 14th century, is also claimed as 'one of the greatest building blunders' to have survived from the Middle Ages '. . . and has entailed endless expense upon successive generations'. There is speculation that this additional structure caused the fall or ruin of the north-west transept, aggravated perhaps by ringing the bells. As early as the beginning of the 15th century the internal arches at the base of the tower had to be reinforced.

In October 1541 it was thought that representations of the Blessed Virgin Mary and the saints might be worshipped in churches, so Bishop Goodrich issued the order that 'all Images . . . Ornaments, Writtings, Table-Monuments . . . Shrynes' etc be destroyed with as much speed as possible. So today, almost certainly due to this order and not through Commonwealth destruction, damage is evident in Bishop West's Chapel, at the east end of the Cathedral and in the Lady Chapel, where almost all human heads except those in the roof bosses were hacked off and most of the stained glass destroyed. Ironically Bishop Goodrich's fine memorial in the south choir aisle is one of the few floor brasses to survive.

During the disturbances of the Civil War, Oliver Cromwell, who had for a while lived in Ely, called on Mr Hitch, Precentor of the Cathedral, to stop 'unedifying and offensive' choir services. Mr Hitch took no action so Cromwell, with a party of soldiers, went to the Cathedral and commanded him to 'leave off your fooling and come down'; he then turned out the congregation. Although Cromwell did not himself close the building it was closed until 1660, after the Act of 1649 for the abolition of Cathedral Deans and Chapters. Ely's then Bishop, Matthew Wren, was imprisoned in the Tower of London for about 18 years and only released at the Restoration.

James Essex made alterations during the 18th century to the supporting wooden structure, which may have saved the lantern, and also removed the exterior stone pinnacles of the octagon. In the next century, as part of an extensive restoration under Dean George Peacock and directed by Sir George Gilbert Scott, further structural work was carried out and new stone pinnacles replaced the earlier ones. The interior was later re-painted, and stained glass windows, with the initial letters GP incorporated, were placed in the octagon. These windows became unsafe during the gales of early 1990; repair from a 'flying' scaffold within the octagon has now begun.

By 1858 the ceiling of the nave had been boarded and amateur artist Henry Styleman Le Strange of Hunstanton started painting it. He died before he finished, so his friend, Thomas Gambier Parry, painted the six bays to the east in a more elaborate and, at the time, more fashionable style. In this century the timbers above were infested with death watch beetle and treated in 1956 to eliminate the pest. Recently, further conservation was carried out both on the timbers and the painted ceiling.

In 1971/2, 22 miles of scaffolding were erected around the west tower to facilitate a comprehensive programme; the 19th century iron bands were removed and stainless steel rods held in reinforced concrete were inserted to 'knit together' the octagon and the four pinnacles. Workmen from Rattee and Kett, accustomed to working at Ely since 1851, when Mr Rattee of Cambridge had laboured on the choir sub-stalls and the organ, were carried up and down in an electric lift. Occasionally groups of local people used it to view the work, and the City below.

It was partly this work and its escalating cost that led to the £4 million appeal for the third great restoration. Launched on 20 September 1986, the Ely Cathedral Restoration Trust raised this large sum of money, much given by East Anglians, in just over a year. The achievement was due to the commitment of Dean Patterson and the Chapter, to the lead given by a professional fund-raising team and to the hard work of many individuals. Directed by Surveyor to the Fabric Peter Miller, Rattee and Kett started work during 1987 to renew the lead on the nave roof; many supporting timbers were replaced, stonework repaired and renewed and other essential work carried out. Fortunately money was also available from other sources so that, while safety scaffolding was up in the nave, the dirt from a century's use of solid-fuel stoves (now converted to gas) was removed from the 19th century painted ceiling.

The Lady Chapel closed to the public in 1988, for re-roofing, restoration of the four corner pinnacles and the windows. With the exception of installation of a panel of surviving mediaeval stained glass, the work was completed at the end of January 1990; part of the Candlemas Service on 2 February was held in the chapel. By day it is now full of clear, bright light and at night can be illuminated to suit a variety of occasions. Some external work had been carried out in the 1950s including new gargoyles, so the stone heads of Dean Carey, four canons and two vergers – some bespectacled – are aloft on the north side. Work on the south transept began in 1989 and was completed in the early months of 1990.

Following the £4 million appeal, the Dean and Chapter launched a '21st Century Fund' to ensure future conservation. Meanwhile, a more controversial measure was necessary to meet the cost of keeping the Cathedral open; on 1 March 1986 an admission charge of £1.50 (increased three times by 1990) was introduced for visitors from outside the City. Of course, there is no charge at times of services or on Sundays, nor for entry to St Catherine's chapel inside the west door, which is available for private prayer whenever the Cathedral is open.

Many additions and changes have taken place inside the building over the centuries. The remains of the extensive painted decorations were covered by washes of white and ochre, later removed; memorials and tombs have been added and the choir has been moved from a central position to the east end and then back westward to its present position. Among early additions were the chantry chapels of Bishop Alcock (15th century) and Bishop West (16th century) at the eastern end of the north and south choir aisles. In both chapels the local stone, clunch, has been elaborately carved. In Bishop Alcock's Chapel, representations of a pun on his name can be seen in glass and stone. Both chapels have interesting ceilings; the earlier is fan vaulted and Bishop West's shows Italian influence, with two remarkable bosses, each with descending angels who carry the coat of arms of the diocese. Incorporated in the carving in Bishop West's Chapel is a Latin motto which translates 'By the Grace of God I am what I am'. When this chapel was brought back into use after about 400 years a reredos and later (1947) the stained glass east window, both designed by Sir Ninian Comper, were placed in the chapel by students of Ely Theological College. Almost all stained glass windows in the Cathedral today are 19th century. In earlier times, before the windows were glazed, some were probably filled with canvas bought, it is recorded, at Lynn; as with many of the Victorian windows, relatively little light would have been admitted.

In the north transept are two small chapels; the most northerly, dedicated to St George, is a memorial to over 5,000 men from Cambridgeshire and the Isle of Ely who lost their lives in World War I. The second chapel is dedicated to St Edmund. The standards hanging above in the aisle are mostly those of local regiments, though two small ones are of the Grenadier Guards and the large ensign is from HMS *Walpole*. The French armour above dates to the Battle of Waterloo, when it was captured. The north-west corner of this transept had become ruinous and was probably rebuilt during the 17th century. Also in this transept is the entrance to the national Stained Glass Museum, opened in 1979 in the triforium. Nearby, in the north presbytery aisle, is the Bomber Command window which commemorates men of 2, 3, 8 and 10 Groups, stationed near Ely in the 1940s.

In the south transept is the Chapel of St Dunstan, where the window is filled with fragments of mediaeval stained glass. This is part of what was once the Cathedral library; the books and chapter records were transferred to the University Library at Cambridge in 1970. The rest of the area is used as a Brass Rubbing and Education Centre. The angel roofs in both transepts date from the 15th century and were repainted as part of the restoration of the 19th century.

It is astonishing that so much building happened during the 14th century. Not only were the Lady Chapel and octagon built then, but also the great gateway known as the Porta, the monastic barn, part of the north range on the south side of the High Street, the church of St Cross or Holy Cross, the Queen's Hall and Prior Crauden's Chapel and study. The Queen's Hall was apparently built to provide a place in which distinguished visitors such as Edward III's queen, Philippa, could be entertained, and was linked by a first-floor corridor to the chapel and the Prior's study. There is a superb mediaeval tiled floor and interesting remains of mural paintings, one of which shows a scene of the Crucifixion, another the Annunciation. The chapel survived, although during 1649 'the building was . . . ordered to be taken down, and sold as old materials, it escaped destruction by being turned into a dwelling-house'. It was re-opened as a chapel in July 1858. Over one hundred years later, further restoration and conservation was carried out; now Prior Crauden's Chapel is a place of quietness and beauty, the gem of the monastic buildings.

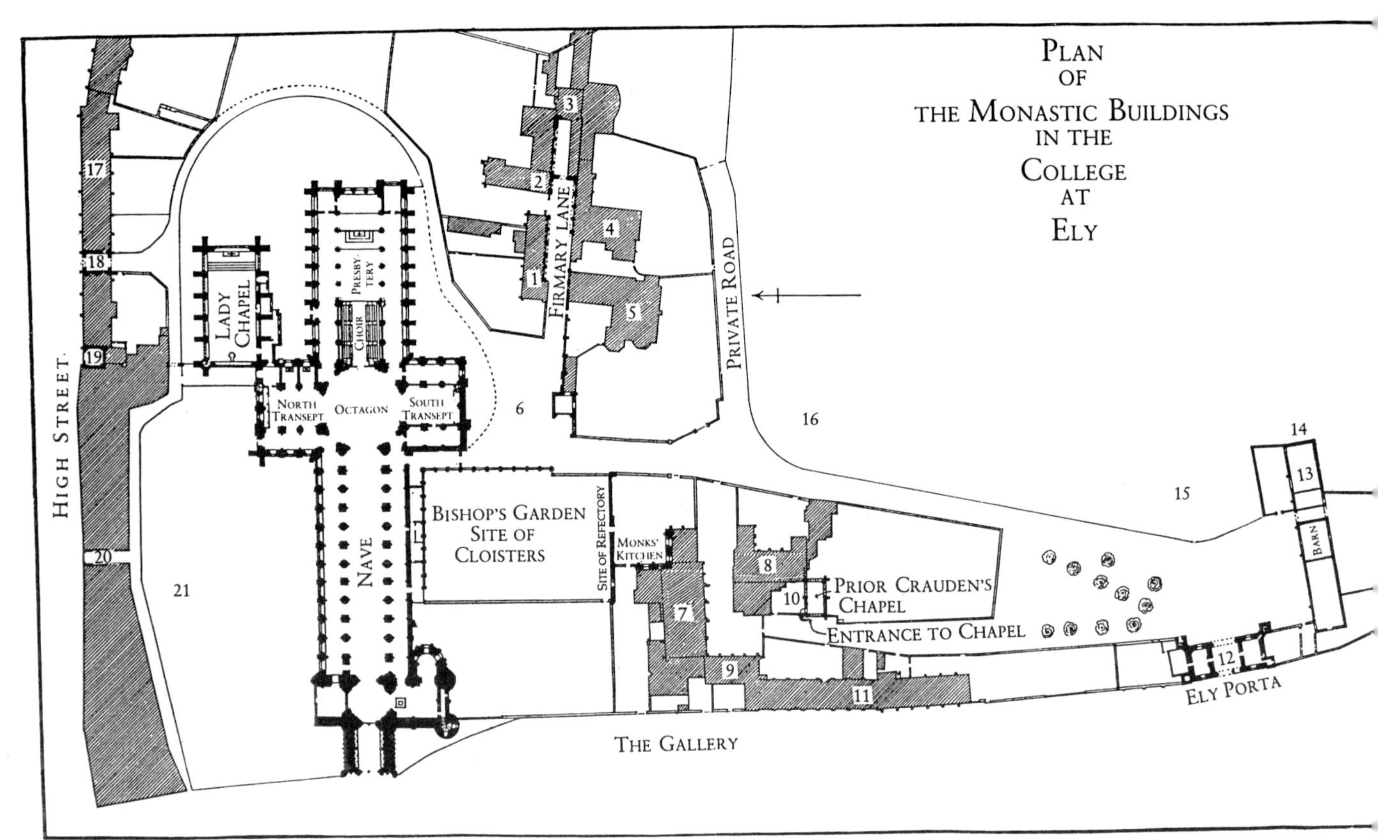

ABOVE: Plan of Cathedral and monastic area; the property of The Dean and Chapter extends further east to the back of properties facing onto Broad Street. 1 Powcher's Hall. 2 The 'Painted' Chamber. 3 The Infirmary Chapel/Chapter House. 4 The Black Hostelry. 5 The Canonry. 6 Site of mediaeval Chapter House, St Catherine's Chapel and monks' dormitory. 7 Great Hall/Bishop's House. 8 The Priory. 9 Queen's Hall. 10 Prior Crauden's Chapel. 11 Servants' quarters/dormitory. 12 The Porta. 13 Monastic Barn/Dining-hall. 14 Cherry Hill. 15 The Park. 16 The Dean's Field or Meadow. 17 The Almonry. 18 Sacrist's Gate. 19 Bell Tower. 20 Steeple Gate. 21 Cross Green. (DC) LEFT: 'The unmutilated view' of the west front. This is a 19th century imaginary view showing both western transepts in a complete state. RIGHT: B. Winkles engraved this print of the west front in 1840.

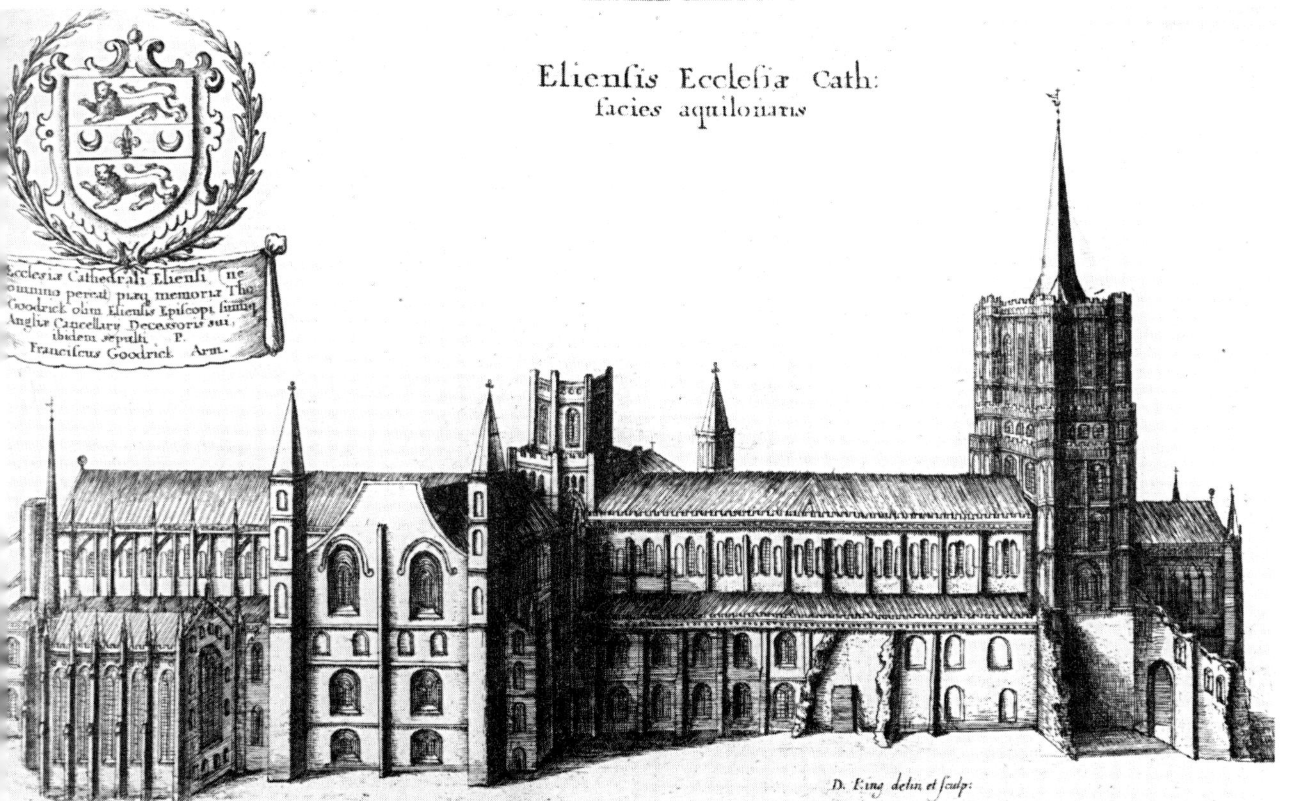

LEFT: The 12th century Prior's doorway was engraved by W. Woolnoth in 1834. The side columns contain signs of the Zodiac and the 'Labours of the Month.' RIGHT: Two men in a boat can be seen at the base on the east side of the door. BELOW: A view from the north engraved by Daniel King from his drawing for the *Monasticon Anglicanum* (1655) shows the pre-Essex Octagon, a small spire (demolished 1801) on the west tower, the remains of Holy Cross Church at the north side of the nave and, to the west, the ruined north west transept. (SAL)

LEFT: The initial letter from Henry VIII's charter of 10 September 1541. (UL) RIGHT: B. Winkles' engraving of 1840 shows the nave before the present floor was laid and before the nave was ceiled. BELOW: The pulpitum is reconstructed in this drawing from James Essex's sketches by William St John Hope. (CC)

ABOVE: Firmary Lane 1808: Powcher's Hall is on the north side, on the south the Black Hostelry. The present Chapter House, once the Infirmary Chapel, is at the far end. BELOW: The Almonry undercroft, after many years as part of a canon's residence is to be opened as a tea room and restaurant in 1990.

ABOVE LEFT: The Galilee Porch: in this Winkles engraving 1840 the great wooden doors have not yet been refaced with 19th century wood and decorative work. RIGHT: The organ and choir stalls are in the presbytery in this Winkles' engraving. There was then no 19th century carving above the stalls by Mr Abeloos of Louvain. Below is a fine collection of mediaeval misericord seats. BELOW LEFT: 'Ely imps you see, Pickaback imps in glee . . .' where two arches meet on the south side of the choir. RIGHT: There are many heads of grotesques and animals but, apart from the roof bosses, only one complete human head, perhaps of the master mason. Hidden behind a grotesque, it is seen here through a mirror.

The interior of the Lady Chapel in 1816; between the arches are sculptured scenes based on the life and legends of the Virgin; it is these figures that were mutilated in the 16th century. The stone vault, with many carved bosses, is the widest of its date in the country. Some artistic licence has been used in this print as there is no sign of the Chapel's use as a parish church.

the Right Hon.ble Thomas Earl of Kinnoul, Chancellor of the Dutchy & County Palatine of Lancaster, & one of his Majesty's most Hon.ble Privy
This Section of the Cathedral Church of Ely from East to West, engraved at his expense, is most gratefully inscribed by James

OPPOSITE ABOVE: This cross-section, 1762, gives some idea of the construction; the arrangement of the structural timbers was modified by both Essex and Scott. The angle columns of the lantern, formed from oak tree trunks about 20m high and estimated to weigh ten tons, were found at 'Chykissand' in Bedfordshire and brought to Ely by water. LEFT: This painting c1796 by J.M.W. Turner looks to the north east. It shows the wooden vault before it was re-painted in the 19th century. References to the original painting of this area state that 'Walter the painter was employed for 42 weeks' and that 'silver foil, gold leaf, vermilion' were used. The new choir screen was designed by Essex. (AAG) RIGHT: The lift-size boss of Christ in Glory in the centre of the lantern vault was carved in wood by John of Burwell for 2s and 'his keep at the Prior's table'. ABOVE: An engraving made from a drawing by J.M.W. Turner, published 1833, shows the Cathedral from the south; note the clear depiction of the 'Essex' lantern. The houses have either been demolished or drastically altered.

ABOVE: Bishop Goodrich's memorial. BELOW: Bishop Matthew Wren. RIGHT: Henry Styleman Le Strange is said to have based his design for the nave ceiling on one he had seen in a church at Hildersheim, Germany, but Dean Harvey Goodwin, in his *Ely Gossip* (1892) says Le Strange told him that he had not been to Germany 'when he conceived the design'. (Top three panels by Thomas Gambier Parry.) (BL)

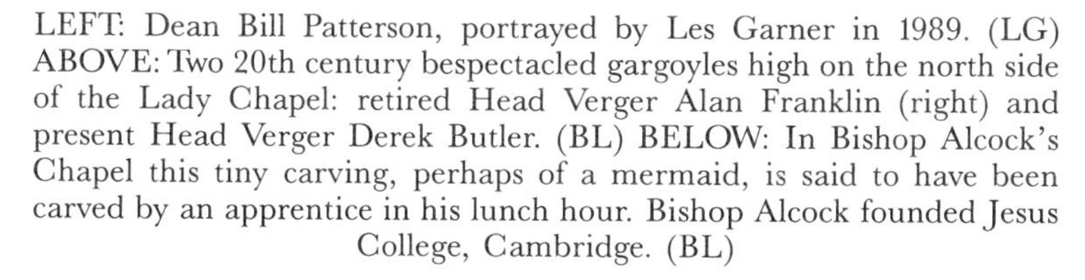

LEFT: Dean Bill Patterson, portrayed by Les Garner in 1989. (LG) ABOVE: Two 20th century bespectacled gargoyles high on the north side of the Lady Chapel: retired Head Verger Alan Franklin (right) and present Head Verger Derek Butler. (BL) BELOW: In Bishop Alcock's Chapel this tiny carving, perhaps of a mermaid, is said to have been carved by an apprentice in his lunch hour. Bishop Alcock founded Jesus College, Cambridge. (BL)

ABOVE: High on the north wall of St Edmund's Chapel is a 12th or 13th century painting of the 870 martyrdom by the Danes of this East Anglian king and saint; there are also traces of painting in imitation of wall hangings on both north and south walls. (BL) BELOW: All buildings in this print of 1845 remain today. In addition to the Prior's prison, the manorial court room was in the Porta, above the main arch. The Manor of Ely Barton, and of Ely Porta, were the two manors in the city. OPPOSITE ABOVE: The east end of Prior Crauden's Chapel and part of the Priory; the Queen's Hall is further to the left (19th century). LEFT: The interior of Prior Crauden's Chapel 1863 looking east; the wooden vaulted ceiling is part of the 19th century restoration. RIGHT: A plan of the tiled pavement in Prior Crauden's Chapel was published in 1801 by W. Fowler. The Adam and Eve panel is in front of the altar. (SAL)

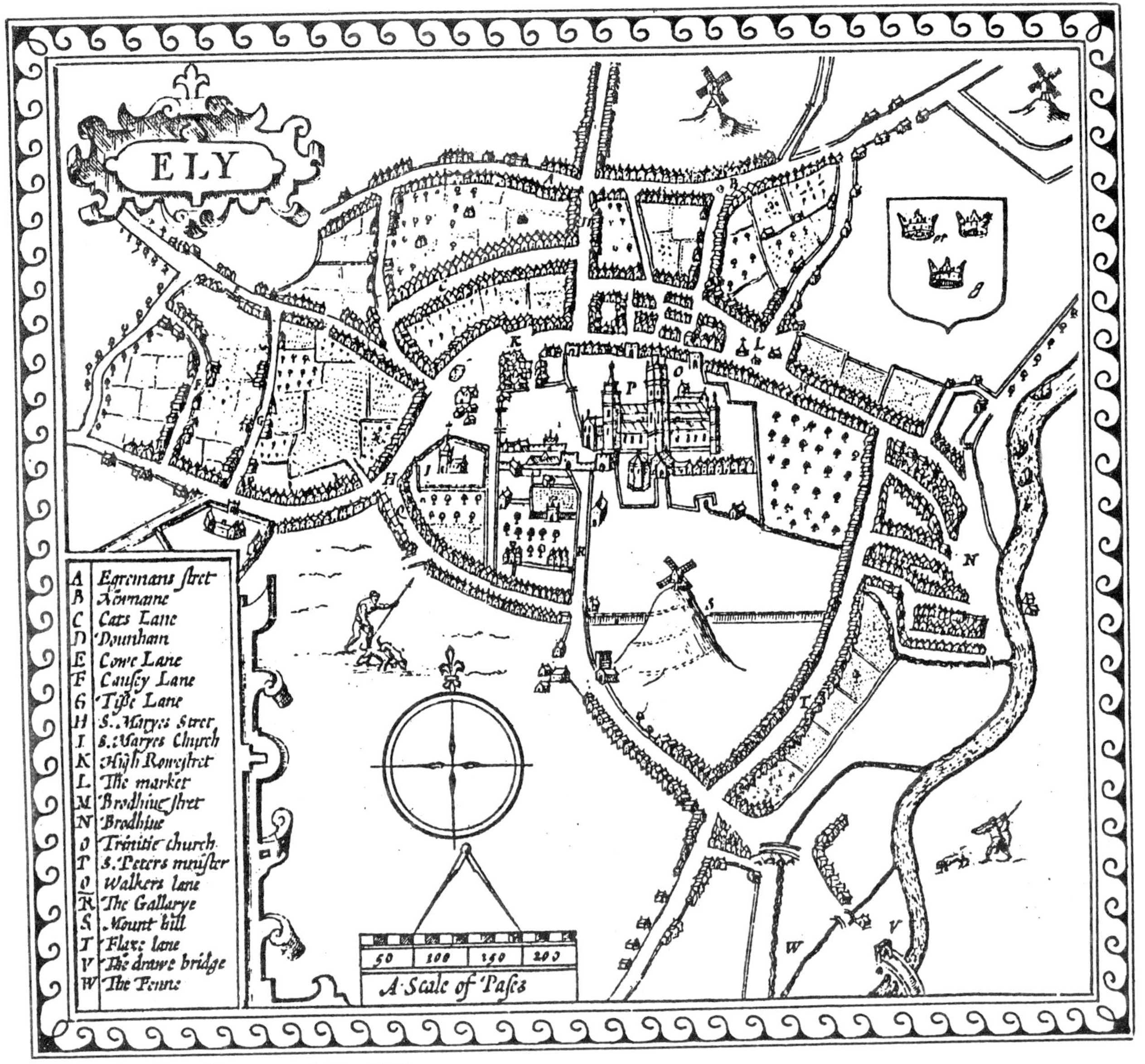

John Speed's map of Ely 1610:

KEY: 1990 followed by 1610 (in CAPITALS) and earlier (in italics where relevant).

Egremont Street, A EGREMANS STRET, *Akermanstrete 1417;* Newnham Street, B NEWNAME; Chapel Street, C CATS LANE, *Catteslane 1417;* Lynn Road, D DOUNHAM, *S(c)henteforthlane 1280 (perhaps Nutholt Lane);* West Fen Road, E COWELANE; Little (Hills) Lane, F CAUSEY LANE; Chiefs Street, G TISSE LANE; St Mary's Street, H S. MARYES STRET; St Mary's Church, I S MARYES CHURCH; High Street, K HIGH ROWE STRET *le Heyrow c1357, Le Hyesstrete 1478 or alternative; for High Street;* Market Place, L THE MARKET, *Le Marketstede 1332;* Fore Hill, M BRODHIVE STRET; Quayside, N BRODHIVE, *Bradehide c1210 le Brodhyth 1390;* Lady Chapel, O TRINITIE CHURCH; The Cathedral, P S PETERS MINISTER; Silver Street, Q WALKERS LANE *Swanlewelane 13th c., Walpol(es)lane 1331;* The Gallery, R THE GALLARYE, *le Galelylane 1438;* Cherry Hill, S MOUNT HILL; Broad Street, T FLAXE LANE, *Brodlane 1280;* Ely High Bridge, V THE DRAWE BRIDGE; Caudwell Fen?, W THE FENNE.

MARKET STREET — Gaol Street 1830, BARTON ROAD — Smockmill Alley and Gaol Lane, CAMBRIDGE ROAD — Stanweye 1319, Bugg's Hill, NUTHOLT LANE — S(c)henteforthlane 1280 Redcrosslane (or Lynn Road), ANNESDALE — Auntresdale 1418, BACK LANE — Flexe Lane, HYTHE LANE — Baldock's Lane, Little Lane, SHIP LANE — Winfarthing Lane (part of) and Barker's Lane, VICTORIA STREET — New Street, LISLE LANE — Lyldeslane 1280 Bull Lane 1840 to c1955, then Lisle Lane. Note that a cross, which may be symbolic only, is shown on the Market Place; there are 18th c references which name a Market Cross as a place on which notices were displayed.

Beyond the College

Henry VIII's 'King's New College at Ely' is remembered in the name by which the area around the Cathedral is known, often in other places called the Close. The name Ely is derived from the Saxon word *elge* – island, willow place or eel district; all appropriate, but the latter most likely.

An Act was passed in 1836 'for the extinguishing of the secular jurisdiction of the bishop of Ely . . .'. Ely gaol, the Bishop's Gaol, was abolished and the Isle became in some ways a division of Cambridgeshire. In 1888 it was changed to form a separate administrative county and six years later the City of Ely Urban District Council succeeded the former Board of Health; the College remained an extra-parochial entity until 1933. The first meeting of the UDC took place in January 1895 under chairman Charles Bidwell and the last early in 1974. Since then Ely has had a City of Ely Council with parish status and a Mayor and Mayoress. Still part of the parish are the hamlets of Queen Adelaide, Prickwillow with an area to beyond Shippea Hill station, Chettisham and Stuntney; it occupies about one square mile with a population of around 11,000. The City's early growth was gradual and one presumes there was little reason for people to settle there unless they served the monastery or were in some way linked with it.

The Domesday Survey was followed by others, including one of 1250. This gave an extensive list of freemen, among whom were residents 'Beyond the Water', an area later known as Babylon. It was probably during the 13th century that the course of the river was altered to flow approximately in its present position. The old course at the foot of Stuntney hill is marked by a rodden, the silt bed of a former river; many show as 'low, light-coloured banks winding across the fens'. The built-up area extended to the south-east beyond the river, and houses at Babylon were occupied until about 1930. More tangible 13th century evidence that Ely had grown, and was expected to grow further, was provided by the rebuilding of St Mary's Church, probably on the site of an earlier building.

By the time of Bishop Fordham's survey of 1417 Ely had developed to the west and north and towards the river on the eastern side. There was also a small area known as Little London, less than a mile from the City centre, near the Tinker of Ely and close to the present Rifleman's Arms on the Lynn Road. Occasionally a building is known to occupy the same site today, as for example Steeple Gate in High Street. In Fordham's survey many tradesmen are listed but no titled persons, esquires or gentlemen. Soon after the Reformation, the population of Ely, given perhaps for the first time in the 1566 survey, was about 1,700. The 'Commonwealth' Survey of 1649 reported on and gave valuations of properties which belonged to the Dean and Chapter, many of which the State proposed to appropriate or destroy. Although it only covered part of Ely, a small number of residents were by that time listed as esquires, gent and Mr, for example, Luke Voyce gent (draper), Mr John Angier, John Goodrich, Oliver Cromwell and Anthony Page esquires, members of the Austin family as gent, Thomas and Robert Steward Esq and also Lady Grace Steward. The Stewards, related to Oliver Cromwell, later to be Lord

Protector of England, farmed at nearby Stuntney. Of the Page family, Anthony was 'Steward of the Court of Ely and . . . all other Courts belonging to the late Dean and Chapter of Ely'. Members of this family continued prominent citizens; Jonathan, the last 'farmer' of the tithes (he organised their collection), lived at Cromwell House; a Thomas Page held office as Sheriff of the County in the 1830s and was associated with Parson's and Needham's charities, with the Local Board of Health and with the Bedford Level Corporation.

On the 1610 John Speed map many of the central streets appear, as today, on the same plan suggested by the 1417 survey. The only area of appreciable growth was in the north-west, near the present Chief's Street and Hills Lane, shown by Speed as Tisse Lane and Causey Lane.

The more detailed Bullis Survey in 1679 of the Manor of Ely Porta shows that many residents held more than one property and also named two titled persons, the Lady Norton and Lady Skipworth; this does not necessarily mean either of them lived in Ely. Names of prominent residents noted in 1649 recur: Austin, Aungier, Goodwriche, Voyce etc.

The 1798 Land Tax records indicate, as most previous and later records confirm, that never more than a handful of either the wealthy or the titled lived in the City. The only persons who paid tax in two figures were Edmund Tattersall Esq of New Barns Farm, William Layton, occupant of property owned by one John Morley, and Jonathan Page Esq. Others who paid a smaller rent, but higher than average in Ely, were farmers Robert Martin at Bedwell Hay Farm, William Hanchett at Braham Farm and Granado Pigott, probably at Barton Farm. Many surnames are familiar in the records of the 18th and 19th centuries such as those of Archer, Bagge, Bentham, Marshall, Dench, Cropley, Chevell, Cuttris, Genn, Greaves, Gotobed, Hall, Harlock, Gisgard, Kempton, Knowles, Luddington, Muriel and Waddington.

Although many streets shown on Speed's map remain today, the position and number of houses shown is largely symbolic, as may be confirmed from the large scale (one inch to 45 ft) 1851 map drawn by estate agent Charles Bidwell. Here coach houses, barns, stables etc, as well as houses are indicated; they cover little more than the area of the Speed map except that development is shown to the south-west where, by that time, a new Turnpike road to Cambridge had been built. In 1841 the population of Ely with Stuntney and Chettisham was 6,825, an increase of about 600 since the previous census. Twenty years later it had risen by about 1,000; there was a slight decline for a while at the beginning of the 19th century but after that a steady increase. Gardener's *Directory* (1851) lists few as lady or gentleman, that description now linked to income; for example Mary Scrundamore and Mary Price Mitchell, annuitant, are both shown as 'lady' with an income from interest of money, the Rev Solomon Smith's sister is the only 'gentlewoman' listed and she, with Mary Scrundamore, had come to Ely from elsewhere.

With so few wealthy citizens the number of important houses are correspondingly few; those rated at £30 per annum were 34 in 1847. Outside the College, one of the earliest of these larger ones to survive is a former merchant's house in Broad Street. It is known, because of its 19th century use as a public house, as the Three Blackbirds. At Crown Point, in the main thoroughfare from river to Market Place, there is another house, also perhaps that of a merchant; here or in an earlier one on the same site, Oliver Cromwell signed his name on appointment as a governor of Parson's Charity, 30 August 1636. That year, he inherited property and the post of Farmer of the Tithes from his maternal uncle, Sir Thomas Steward, and came to live in the house next to St Mary's Church, known today as Oliver Cromwell's House. His daughter, Frances, was baptised at St Mary's Church in 1638 during the four to five years when his home was in Ely. Here, it is suggested, was the setting for Andrew Marvell's lines:

> 'From his private gardens, where
> He lived reservèd and austere
> As if his highest plot
> To plant the bergamot.'

Whether this referred to the herb or the pear tree, one of the latter was still in the walled garden before the new Vicarage was built in 1989. Cromwell's family apparently lived in the city, either in this house or elsewhere, until 1647. After Jonathan Page died in 1843 it was sold to Joseph Rushbrook, who soon opened it as the Cromwell Arms, at first only licensed to sell ale. It was plastered over to be given its present appearance, in 1905. Thenceforth it was St Mary's Vicarage, until 1986 when it was bought by the East Cambridgeshire District Council as a Tourist Information Centre, due to open in June 1990. Behind wooden panelling a fine example of painted imitation panelling c1600 has been found. Nearby was the sacrist or sextry barn used to store the tithes, when a tenth of the parish produce was collected in kind; after the Tithe Act of 1836, payment was converted to cash. The barn fell into a ruinous state and was demolished; part of the site was used when Thomas Parson's Square, a group of almshouses, was built in 1844 with money from Parson's Charity. Architect George Basevi, who was also responsible for the FitzWilliam Museum in Cambridge, fell to his death a year later from scaffolding inside the west tower of the Cathedral, and was buried in the north choir aisle.

To the other side of Oliver Cromwell's House lies the present St Mary's Church, built under Bishop Eustace early in the 13th century. Its growth, like that of the City, was gradual. The oldest parts are the chancel and nave; the north porch, probably built as the City developed in that direction, and also the west tower and spire, are 14th century. St Mary's was restored in 1829 and again in 1876; several alterations were made to the roofs and the nave ceiling was painted. Little of the present furniture is old, though the church retains its parish chest, complete with three locks. The side chapel provides a link with the former parish for, since 1942, it has been known as Holy Trinity Chapel. To the south a new hexagonal parish room, built for £60,000, can be reached either through the re-opened south door or outside by passing to the west of the tower. The room was opened on 27 April 1985 by Eric Goodrich, who had been churchwarden for 20 years, and the former parish hall, built in 1891 in Cambridge Road, was sold.

St Peter's, a Chapel of Ease designed by J.P. St Aubyn, was built in Broad Street in 1889 by Catherine Maria Sparke, to commemorate her husband, Canon Edward Bowyer Sparke, and to accommodate the needs of the increased population of the area. It was dedicated on 30 June 1890. Now, administered by a body of Trustees, it has a small, faithful congregation who arranged special services and a Flower Festival to mark the centenary in 1989.

Bedford House in St Mary's Street was almost certainly the largest and most important privately owned house in Ely when it was built about 1800, on the site of earlier tenements. Thomas Page lived there and it was perhaps his son, another Thomas, who sold the property in 1844 to the 'Governors, Bailiffs and Commonalty of the Corporation of the Conservators of the Great Level of the Fens called Bedford Level'. The building was the Corporation's headquarters for 20 years, until bought by Joseph Little JP, when it once again became the residence of a family of some consequence in the City. Its use changed yet again when the High School for Girls opened there in 1905. It was restored in 1989 and, with the rest of the site, developed by the Cambridge Housing Society Ltd as a sheltered housing development of flats for rent. On the ground floor of the main house is the Bedford House Day Centre where the room recently known as the Conference Room and once used by the Bedford Level Corporation and the High School among many local organisations, is sometimes available for community use.

Of other buildings, the former Bishop's Palace is the largest. Perhaps the most interesting are those at St John's Farm. The Palace, begun in Bishop Alcock's time in the 15th century was much extended in the two succeeding centuries and has 'a more complicated history and a greater number of architectural problems than any other building in Ely'. The interior was remodelled by Bishop Keene in 1771 though much of the chapel decoration dates from 1884 and later. The garden is extensive and the plane tree, said to have been planted by Bishop Gunning in 1674, is reputedly the largest in England, perhaps in Europe. At a time when Ely

Bishops were of importance as advisers to the monarch, as ambassadors, as chancellors of Oxford and of Cambridge Universities, and as Masters of Colleges, they had 10 residences. During the 14th century these were at Ely, Little Downham, Somersham, Wisbech and Doddington within the Isle of Ely but also at Hadham, Bishops Hatfield, Balsham, Fen Ditton and at Ely Place, Holborn in London. After 1722 the London residence was at Dover Street but the name Ely Place remains in Holborn and the church there is dedicated to St Etheldreda. From 1940 the Bishop of Ely no longer lived at the Palace but made his home at the former Deanery, once the great hall of the monastery, on the opposite side of The Gallery. This is a large, partly 14th century, structure over a 13th century undercroft.

The group of buildings at St John's Farm are thought to be the remains of the Hospitals of St John and St Mary Magdalen and, although little is known of their history, records show that the two were united in 1240. 'By the ordinance of Bishop Northwold, the united hospital was to consist of 13 chaplains and brethren, who were to have a common refectory and dormitory, and to wear a uniform habit; they were to be under the immediate government of the Sacrist of Ely'. A 1327 tax return refers to 'The Master of the Hospital of St John' as paying 'xs jd' and later a fire occurred there. In the 16th century, when its last Master was also Master of Clare Hall, Cambridge (as it was then known), the ownership of the area, with other property in the City was transferred to Clare; nearby Clare Cottages are a reminder. By 1908 there were 'scarcely any remains of the buildings' and today the two most extensive are part of St John's Farm. The estate was bought by Mrs Runciman in 1925 and her descendents remain there today.

Another two dozen substantial houses are to be found in Ely, most no earlier than 17th century, though some have older 'cores'. Few houses of any size were pulled down to make way for these and records confirm there has been little destruction by fire. The only rebuilding on any scale in the City centre for several hundred years was that on the Market Place and near the junction of Nutholt Lane with Lynn Road. On the Market Place the Sessions House was demolished to make way for the Corn Exchange. This in turn, with the Public Room, was demolished to make way for a new shopping area which opened in 1966.

There are, of course, smaller houses, mostly timber-framed, which have survived, and in the mediaeval heart of the City many buildings are older than would appear at first glance. For example, that once occupied by Harvey's, the drapers in High Street to the west of High Street Passage, premises east of Steeple Gate, those on the corner of St Mary's Street known as Mepsale's, later Gouldstone's, and so on. Of the smaller houses, the one that attracts most attention is the much-restored timbered house to the east of St Mary's Church, bounded on the west by Lardner's Lane, on the east by Church Lane. Perhaps the most important are the cottages at the eastern end of Silver Street, part of which once formed an open hall with two cross wings; the properties belong to the Cambridgeshire Cottage Improvement Society. During restoration in 1989, 14th and 16th century wall painting were found, and on the first floor 'the main hall truss with its crown post', previously hidden. Another mediaeval timbered cottage is that in Broad Street, opposite the gates of The Park.

These older buildings, even those of the 19th century, were erected in a City which was much less comfortable to live in than that of today. The poor suffered severely from lack of amenities and everyone found rough, ill-paved, dirty streets with little or no lighting, overcrowded cemeteries, an unsatisfactory water supply and only rudimentary fire and police services. Intrepid horsewoman Celia Fiennes, who visited Ely during her 1698 journey, described the City as 'the dirtyest place I ever saw . . . the streets . . . a perfect quagmire . . .' and still by 1830 only one street was paved, 'the rest very dirty'. Sanitary conditions a little over a hundred years ago were appalling by present-day standards, as is shown in the *Preliminary Inquiry into the*

Sewerage, Drainage, and Supply of Water and the Sanitary Condition of the Inhabitants (1850) by William Lee. Public roads were evidently gravelled by the mid-19th century and, though many footpaths were flagged with York stone (5s 10d per square yard), most courtyards were unpaved. These conditions made the recommended form of cleaning (that the ground be 'watered, washed, and cleansed with flexible hose and jets of water') impossible to implement. Even as recently as 1913 it was said that the road surface in Market Street had been 'covered with flints' and no attempt made to roll them in, but a photo of High Street taken about the same time shows a tarmacadam road between level pavements. Today Lynton Close and Upherd's Lane remain 'unadopted' in spite of recommendations as far back as 1930 that the latter be 'taken over'.

By February 1836 the principal streets were lighted by gas, the lamps 'placed upon elegant painted cast-iron pillars', at which the inhabitants were 'much pleased and satisfied'; a party was held at the White Lion to celebrate the introduction of gas to St Mary's Parish where, in St Mary's Street, there were 11 lamps. Trinity Parish had 52, the College 16; nevertheless 'several parts of the town' were not lighted. The Gas-works of 1835 was said to be one of the few in the Kingdom to belong to an individual and by 1850 two gasometers had been built on Station Road. Improvement was slow, though in August 1854 'the darkness of the venerable city was changed into brilliant light'. The possibility of an electricity supply in Ely was talked of in 1913 and, although this became a reality within two years, the streets continued to be lighted by gas until 1955. The 'Switch On' performed by UDC chairman W. Ruane on 7 October marked the lighting by electricity of the main streets. For a time this was supplied by the Ely Gas and Electricity Co Ltd from the Gas Works, partly rebuilt in 1904 in Station Road. Manufacture of gas stopped in 1958 and was supplied from gasholders at Cambridge, until in 1969 Ely received natural gas.

The cemeteries of St Mary's and Holy Cross became overcrowded by mid-19th century, the position at the latter exacerbated by the 1832 cholera epidemic. This state of affairs must have made body-snatching easier; certainly it was feared, for a watchman was appointed to protect 'the bodies buried'. The need for a new cemetery was confirmed by sexton John Nightingale's report 'I rarely open a grave without finding bones. I have had explosions of gas, and on one occasion I was made sick immediately . . .' The Bishop also expressed his anxiety about the state of the burial ground at Holy Cross and a *Cambridge Chronicle* report said '. . . can anything exhibit a more disgraceful sight or revolting spectacle than a churchyard literally bestrewn with dead mens' skulls or black decayed bones?'. The two churchyards were closed for burial when the new cemetery (cost £3,500) near the present New Barns Road was opened on 12 May 1855. Soon the first adult interment took place and, as the deceased was a Dissenter, on the unconsecrated side. This cemetery (with additional ground) remains in use today.

The cholera epidemic underlined the lack of a good water supply; the high incidence of death in an area where water came from the river perhaps led to earlier action following the 1850 inquiry than might otherwise have been the case. By 1840 two public water conduits existed on Back Hill and there were also three pumps in the streets, but all were kept locked, only to be 'used for watering the roads'; the water was from the river. Most premises obtained hard water from wells, many were without pumps or soft water cisterns; summer proved a difficult time. It was recommended that a constant supply of good water be obtained by levying a weekly rate per house of 'a penny farthing to three half-pence.' Matters appeared to move quickly as the foundation 'stone' of the first water tower was laid by the Dean of Ely in August, 1853. By the next year pipes were laid and owners and occupants of premises were required to apply for connection to the mains, in order to receive water brought through an eight-and-half-mile pipe, from wells in the chalk beds near Isleham to the south-east. This elegant tower was replaced by one of concrete built in 1938/9. Thirty years later the Highflyer tower was built to improve the supply.

In the 1850s pipes to take sewage were laid down and houses were required to have a proper water-closet or privy. The urgent need for both had been made only too clear in Mr Lee's report. He found many localities where the relation of filth to disease was apparent and spoke of offensive ditches, foul privies, cesspools and lack of drainage. 'In Fuller's-yard, Broad Street, there is a privy, manure heap, cowhouse and a stagnant drain with the surface above the floors of some houses adjoining – filth percolates through the wall.' In one house 'the watercloset used by the family' was under the kitchen so, on the rare occasions when the cesspool was emptied, the floor had to be taken up and the 'soil emptied by tubs which two men carry in slings'. It was then 'poured on the street upon a bed of long manure' and loaded into an open cart out of which it 'spilled all along the streets'. In Smock-alley two houses were without privies or water supply and, although overcrowding appears to have been more common in Cambridge, here 12 people had the use of only two bedrooms. Gradually the whole City received a supply of water, and drains were provided, but by 1913 those drains were in need of renewal; in June a Mr Hall said 'the basement of his house had been filled with crude sewage' since April. A £17,000 sewerage scheme was adopted in 1914 but later abandoned. By 1923 the scheme was again vetoed; the estimated cost, £24,800. During the 1940s and '50s a new scheme was discussed but, almost unbelievably, the system was not renewed until the 1960s; a new sewage disposal unit has also been opened.

LEFT: 'Chettisham is a hamlet and chapelry in the parish of Ely St Mary, situate about two miles north west from Ely . . . its population in 1841 was 90' but by 1851 there were only five or six houses and its population was c50. Today there are about 40 houses, a garage, a business park and a small 12th century church. BELOW: 'Prickwillow is a small hamlet in the fens in the parish of Holy Trinity about 4 miles north east of Ely.' The river Lark is crossed by Prickwillow Bridge. St Peter's Church built 1868 is a chapel of ease. RIGHT: The bowl of this marble font is now in Prickwillow Church; it had originally been given to Ely Cathedral by Dean Spencer in 1693.

LEFT: 'Stuntney is a hamlet and chapelry in the parish of Ely Holy Trinity . . . about 1½ miles SE from Ely. Its acreage (2,597) is included with Ely, and its population in 1841 was 220 souls.' The Church of the Holy Cross, almost rebuilt 1876, and shown here 1806, has three Norman arches. CENTRE: Queen Adelaide, here c1900, named after a public house, now closed, to which the name of William IV's Queen had been given, now has no church, post office or shop. Travellers have to cross a rail bridge, river bridge and three railway crossings. RIGHT: 'Burnt Fen, a district containing about 15,000 acres, belonging to the parish of Ely Trinity and Ely St Mary . . . there are two steam engines here . . . engaged on the drainage of the fens,' here in 1851. BELOW: The home of the Steward family at Stuntney; the remains of the group of buildings behind the house can be seen on the east side of the road.

ABOVE: Three boys paddling in the River Ouse; the Merry's house on the left and the Crudgington's to the right, 1910. (CC) BELOW: Steeple Gate was reconstructed in the 16th century over a 14th century undercroft; the measurements of the frontage remain as in the 1417 survey. It is on the site of an earlier entrance to Cross Green, seen here before the 1960s and known as St Peter's Tower.

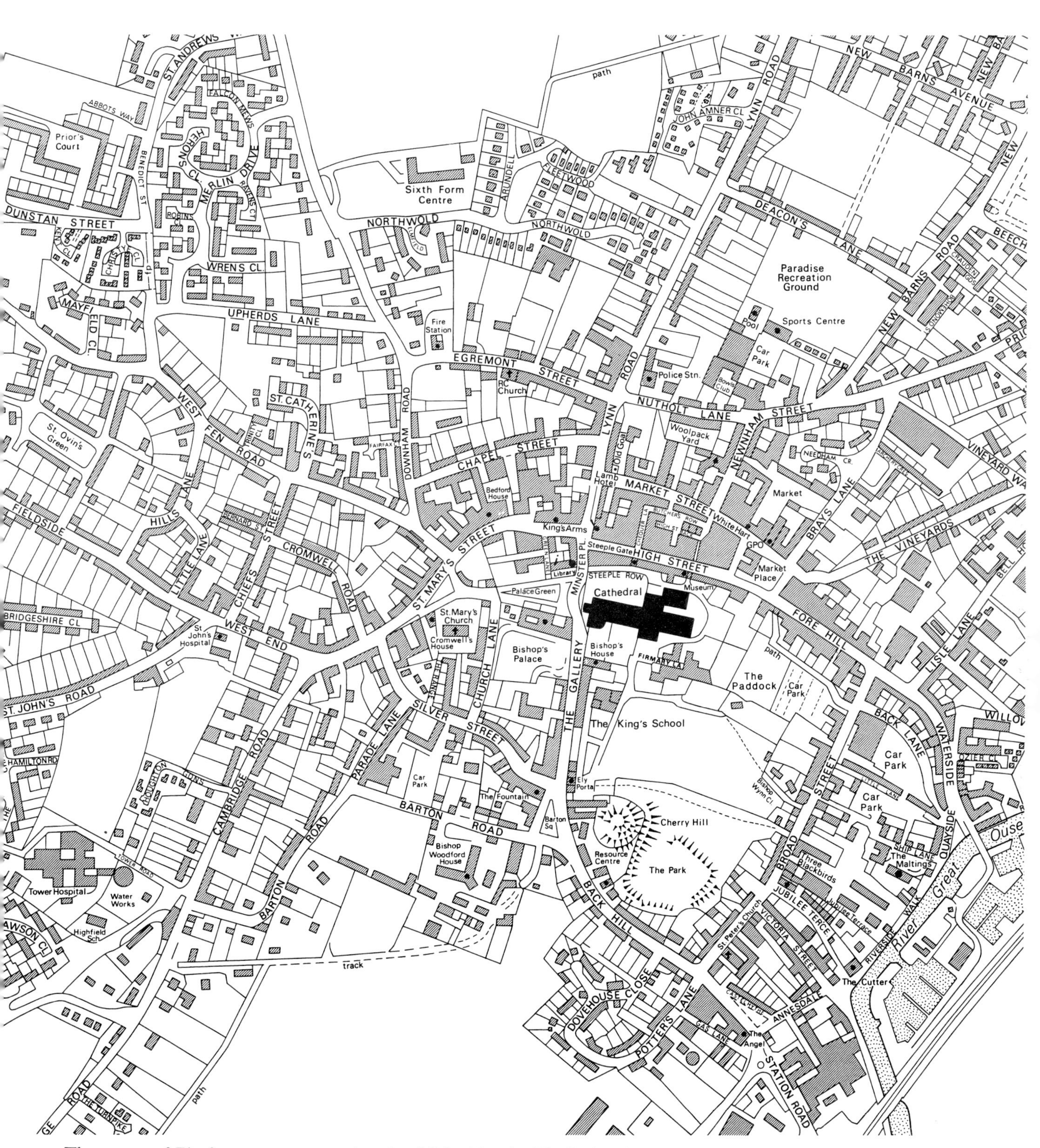

The centre of Ely from a map created and published by the Ely Society in 1975, revised 1986. (ESC)

ABOVE: Restoration by the Ely Preservation Trust of the former Three Blackbirds public house, probably once a merchant's house, was completed in 1984; it now forms three dwellings. Originally built in the 13th century, much of the existing building is 14th century. (JH) BELOW: Smoke-blackened timbers from the middle section of the building date from c1280. Below, a series of hearths, one above the other, were excavated. Towards the river is the part of the building where the merchant probably had his business quarters. Here the roof timbers date from the beginning of the 14th century and are thought to be an early example of this type of construction. (JH)

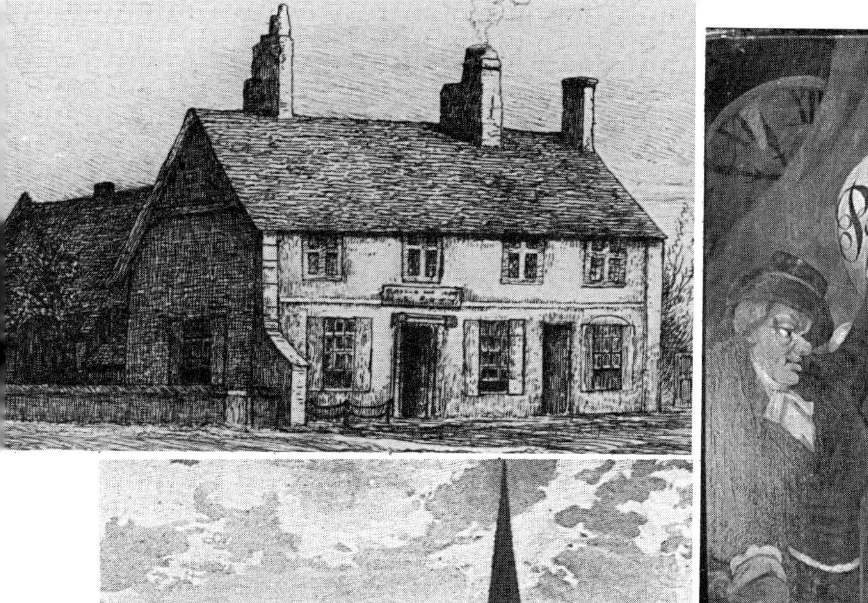

ABOVE: Oliver Cromwell's signature, 1636. (PC) LEFT: The Cromwell Arms 1843-1871, described in the 1649 Parliamentary Survey as 'A fair Parsonage House, built with Brick and Stone, and covered with Tyles, con't a Hall, a Parlor, a Kitchen, Buttery, Larder, Milk-house and other necessary roomes with Chambers over them'. The wing on the left is the oldest part of the surviving house. RIGHT: When the landlord was refused a licence to sell wines and spirits he commissioned local artist and Town Crier John Toombs to paint this sign. It portrays, in caricature, the licensing magistrates Dean Peacock and Rev George Hall with a clock which shows them to be drinking after hours. This caused such a sensation that it was only allowed to hang outside for a short time. (ECDC) BELOW: Oliver Cromwell's House c1870, before the 1905 restoration when it received its present timbered appearance. The almshouses, Thomas Parson's Square, built 1844, are on the right.

ELY, CAMBRIDGESHIRE

VALUABLE FREEHOLD

HOTEL, BREWERY,

AND

BEER-HOUSE,

With Convenient

OUTBUILDINGS & GARDEN,

(The property of Mr. Joseph Rushbrook, who is retiring from business.)

To be Sold by Auction, by

W. B. SPEECHLEY

At The "Cromwell Arms" Hotel, in Ely,

On Thursday, January 21st, 1869, At 6 for 7 o'clock, in the Evening.

(In the following or such other Lots as may be determined upon at the Time of Sale and subject to such Conditions as will be then produced and read.)

LOT 1. All that newly built Brick and Slate, Freehold Beer-House, called the "Fountain" situate at the corner of Silver Street, in Ely, with a frontage of 57 feet 6 inches, containing, cellar, Tap-room, parlour, and kitchen, large dining or club room, and 4 chambers, with yard, stables, and outbuildings, thereto belonging, bounded on or towards the North, by Silver Street; on or towards the East, by Barton Square; on or towards the South, by property of Thomas Bates; and on or towards the West, by property late of Thomas Spooner.

LOT 2. All that old established, well built, Freehold Hotel, called the "Cromwell Arms," situate in Saint Mary's, in Ely, containing 2 cellars, store-room, bar, smokey, large dining room, large kitchen, pantry, Tap-room, and 6 bed rooms: and ALSO ALL THAT 3 quarter brewery, malt chamber, stables, gig-house, and other outbuildings, yard, and capital garden, well planted and walled in, bounded on or towards the North, by Saint Mary's Street; on or towards the East, by Saint Mary's Church; on or towards the South, by the National School; and on or towards the West, by the Alms Houses.

N.B. The Brewing Plant to be taken by Valuation.

For further particulars apply to Mr. Edwin Cross, Solicitor, Ely and Haddenham, or to the Auctioneer, Chief's Street, Ely.

Ely, December 28th, 1868.

W. B. CREAK, PRINTER, ELY

An 1868 bill of sale for the Cromwell Arms and the Fountain.

ABOVE: The Sextry Barn 1797, which was demolished c1843. LEFT: St Mary's Church. The old man on the right is said to be Isaac Aspland, violinist and harpist. RIGHT: The north door, St Mary's Church.

LEFT: St Mary's before the 1876 restoration: the oldest parts are the chancel and nave, the former with 13th century lancet windows and an oddly truncated east window. In the nave are pointed arches with columns and capitals of the Norman period, perhaps from an earlier building. One of the three galleries, all removed 1876, on the right; the three-decker pulpit was later removed. RIGHT: A rood screen 1893, probably Sir Ninian Comper's earliest work, in St Peter's Church in Broad Street, is painted red, green and gold. (BL) BELOW: Bedford House as it was when Joseph Little and his family lived there before 1905. The main part of the building was built c1800.

ABOVE: The Bishop's Palace: a sketch by Henry Rushbury c1930 shows one of the few red brick buildings in the city centre, with dressed stone corners and carved decoration on the north front. LEFT: A Tudor doorway and other remains at Little Downham date from when they were part of 'The pratie palace . . . in the fen', a residence of the Bishops of Ely. The alms of the See of Ely with three crowns is on the left. RIGHT: Today this building is at St John's Farm and, with the barn nearby, was once part of the Hospital of St John and St Mary Magdalen. (CAS)

CITY
HOTEL

OPPOSITE LEFT: The Public Room. (MR) RIGHT: The Corn Exchange, built 1847, survived for over 100 years but was demolished in 1965 when it was sold with the Public Room for £20,000 to City and Suburban Properties. It was replaced by a group of shops. CENTRE: An early 20th century bird's eye view which shows the White Hart, the Temperance Hotel, Martin Hall's House, Archer House and the Market Place, the Corn Exchange and the Public Room. To the left are the lanes, site of the mediaeval butchery, leading from High Street to Market Street. BELOW: Cottages in Broad Street, demolished 1933 to allow the entrance to the timber merchant's premises to be enlarged; in the middle cottage lived a man named Hardy, a fellmonger or dealer in skins. ABOVE: The most impressive painted area in this Silver Street cottage is on the first floor and includes a dove with the words 'Deale Justlye' and a peacock with the words 'Be not Proud' in white on a terracotta background with black outlines and letters. The oldest painting, on the ground floor, is of a vine frieze. (CI and CCIS) BELOW: This small painting (11 inches wide) of High Street by an unknown artist c1840 shows on the left the earlier opening known as Church Way (the Sacrist Gate archway was filled in at the time and was part of a house), the sedan chair used by the Dean's wife and, in the distance, Bedford House. On the right are the Bell Hotel, the Red Lion public house and the extraordinary bay window removed from the facade of Peck's shop in the 1920s.

Peck's has traded in the High Street since before 1893; in 1858 it was on the Market Place.

OPPOSITE LEFT: Henry Baines drew Peck's window c1857. RIGHT: The Gas Works on Station Road; later on this site was Graven's, later Trigon's, garage. (CC) CENTRE: A view up Fore Hill shows an early gas lamp and, from the left, the Glazier's Arms, Lemmon's butcher shop, Tom Bolton's photographer's shop, Blakeman's premises and across the road the premises of Louis King, boot and shoe maker, and Clements, the printers, c1912. BELOW: Ely water tower, built with 618,000 local bricks, considered 'a perfect masterpiece, both in design and workmanship'. ABOVE LEFT: Cross Green in 1817; the majority of the grave stones were removed in 1960. The building to the left of the Lady Chapel was apparently demolished in the 19th century. RIGHT: The Church of England and the Non-Conformist Chapels at Ely Cemetery, engraved 1860, built by Richard Freeman in 1855/6. BELOW: Fuller's Yard, Broad Street by Henry Baines. (MT)

ABOVE: Barges moored near Babylon, probably in the 1920s; the Quay is in the foreground. (CC) BELOW: Newstead's fish shop, once in the Butter Market on the western side of The Market Place. The business closed down 1970 after 83 years in the city. INSET: Newstead's van.

Earning a Living

Evidence in and around Ely, some from about 2,000 BC, shows early man hunted and fished locally. Later the abbey at Ely was kept supplied by nearby farms and fisheries and Ely men had 'to plough, thresh, weed and reap' on abbey lands, providing horses, and transporting provisions for the monks. The Sacrists' Rolls give further information about life and work from the late 13th to mid-14th century; the need to maintain the causeway and bridges between Ely and Stuntney provided work annually for men and in 1323/4 women were also employed. In 1341 payment was made to plumbers, painters and carpenters for working on the causeway at 'Tydbreye and at Brame'; also on the pay roll were the sacrist's groom, stable boy and kitchen boy. A large number were engaged on the monastic buildings, including the cathedral, in particular the 'new work' of the octagon. Few were Ely residents, as craftsmen moved to wherever there was work: many referred to by name indicate this *eg*: John of Burwell, Wulstane of Dalham, and Alan of Walsingham.

The 1327 list of taxpayers gives no indication of occupations but Fordham's survey of the next century refers to many trades. Included were 'bakere', miller, brewer, butcher, cooper, maltster, 'wolleman', webster, tailor, goldsmith, glover, saddler, cowherd, shepherd, thresher and 'schpwryghte'. Apart from the clergy no professional men were listed either in this or in the Commonwealth survey, though in the latter Robert Claxton, cathedral organist, is named.

The river was, and continues to be, a source of income in many ways. There is evidence of trade to and from Lynn in 1566, when in Ely there were 'three barges whereof one belongeth to Thomas Archer, . . . eighte persons which do labor and get theire living with the same, comonlie usynge the caryage of grayne to Lynn'. In the reverse direction tallow, iron, nails and spices among other goods came to Ely. Fish provided an important source of income and food; in the 12th century 'So great a store there is of Fishes that Strangers coming hither make a wonder at it . . . for one halfpenny and under, five men at the least' could not only 'eat to slake hunger and content nature, but also feed their fill of Fishe and Fowle'. Later, when many saw their livelihood threatened by the drainage of the fens, that enterprise nevertheless provided work for other fen folk.

The area near the river has been associated for many years with boat-building; today Babylon on the south side is occupied by a large marina but from the 18th century boat-building by the Ely firms of Cuttriss, Ashberry, Eaves, Pond and Appleyard took place on both sides. 'William Ashberry Begs to aquaint the friends of his late master, Mr. John Pond, that he has taken the BOATWRIGHT BUSINESS so long carried on at Ely by Mr. John Pond, his father and grandfather, and hopes for a continuance of the favours bestowed on them . . . nothing shall be wanting on his part to execute the work as heretofore . . .'. So the business was advertised in the *Cambridge Chronicle* of 1819. Ted Appleyard, the last of a line of seven generations of boat-builders, now over 80, still lives by the river, though the firm ceased to build boats in the 1970s.

Osiers grown at 'holts' on the river near Ely were landed at the several rod yards in the Waterside area; near the back of the former Black Bull, near Common Muckill Bridge and, most photographed, at the river end of the former Three Blackbirds property. This yard was run by William Fear, who had come to Ely from Earith some time before 1871, and whose family kept the link with Earith: described in 1896 as 'John Fear, Basket Manufacturer, and Rod Merchant, Ely' and 'Osier Grower at Ely and Oxlode, Cambs., and Earith, Hunts'. In the 1870s there were about 40 basketmakers living in Ely, more than four times the number 20 years earlier; nearly half had moved to the City from Norfolk and no doubt numbered among the seven men and two apprentices employed by the Scott family. Oliver Scott was the last of a family whose business was said by his father Robert to have been founded 'in the days of Oliver Cromwell'. By 1938, shortly before his death, Mr Scott said 'the trade is absolutely dead'; seventy years earlier Scott baskets had been sold throughout the area, particularly at Bury Market. Basketmaking did not die out completely until the 1960s, with the death of Sam Cox (96) and Jack Hills.

The cloth industry, so important in the adjoining counties of Norfolk and Suffolk, is not often mentioned in Ely's records. The 1417 survey includes a few names suggestive of a cloth trade link: William Wolleman, Agnes Fuller, John and Richard Webstere and Edward Schepherde. For a short time during the 17th century the poor were set to work at spinning and it was agreed in 1675 that Nicholas Wythers of Norwich would employ the 'severall poore persons of the City of Ely in Spinning of Jersey '; the thread was taken to Norwich and Cambridge by pack-horse. It was about then that Thomas Baskerville travelled to Ely and saw sheep 'tumbled into the river within . . . a frame of fir poles'. Again in the 18th century the poor in Holy Trinity Workhouse were required 'to work in Carding, Spinning and Weaving according to their . . . abilities'. The production of woad is recorded; a blue dye presumably linked with cloth-making, though not necessarily in Ely, paupers were employed by Mr Richard Tattersall in 'the woad Businness at Newbarns in 1784'. By 1851 there were few shepherds in Ely and no mention of anyone else involved in cloth-making.

As may be expected from the nature of the land, there is little evidence of extensive early enclosure, inevitably linked as it was near Ely with the drainage of the fens. The Bishop's farm or grange of New Barns was progressively enclosed from the end of the 15th century and eventually included about 700 acres. At Bedwell Hay Farm the enclosure of 120 acres took place before 1548, a comparatively large amount for this area; others took place at Chettisham and Stuntney. 'By the 16th century enclosure became common in the upland parts of the county' mostly to the south and also in the northern silt fens. It continued gradually throughout the 17th century and from 1750 became more general elsewhere, but around Ely, where it had begun on a small scale, it took place later. The Enclosure Act for Ely St Mary is dated August 1848 and the 'Ely St Mary Open Fields Inclosure Map of the New Allotments and of Lands Exchanged 1844' provides a comprehensive record.

Ely citizens continued in subsistence occupations as well as in the repair and alteration of the Cathedral and monastic buildings and, as Daniel and Samuel Lysons record in *Magna Britannia* (1808), 'There is no manufacture in or near the city, except some potteries of coarse ware: many of the inhabitants are employed in the culture of gardens; great quantities of asparagus, and various other vegetables, being sent, by the gardeners in the neighbourhood of Ely, to Cambridge and London. The cherry gardens are extensive; the soil, indeed, seems to have been from a very early period favourable for the growth of fruit; three acres of vineyard at Ely are mentioned in the Domesday Survey: and the anonymous author of a Chronicle of the monastery, which seems to have been written about the year 1368, speaks of these vineyards as being ''in his time very productive'' '. The Lysons' account acknowledges Ely's advantage: goods could be distributed by water to Stourbridge Fair at Cambridge and many other towns.

The 1851 census, the first to give details of occupations, maintains the same view of both the area and the City and is further confirmed by the 1850 Report, which states 'Ely has no manufactures which can materially affect the general health of the place. Coarse pottery and brown earthenware are made from the clay of the district, and tobacco-pipes from clay imported, but very few persons are engaged in these occupations . . .'. In the whole county of Cambridgeshire there were 24,000 agricultural labourers, a figure more than ten times that of any occupation, other than that of farmer, and in Ely 560 labourers, about one in 14 of the population of about 8,000, were employed as agricultural labourers. There were some forty farmers working land varying from 10 to 1,000 acres; at Highflyer Hall on the outskirts of the City to the north-east, Charles Moseley employed thirty men.

John Hall and John Harlock, Ely farmers, were also brewers, the former only farming 200 acres but employing a total of fifty. Ely historian John Beckett writes: 'The brewing and sale of beer was evidently an important part of the economy of Ely for over 700 years, since in the year 1257 King Henry III ordered the Mayor and Burgesses of Lynn . . . to permit the men of Ely to come into their town and sell their ale without let or hindrance'. On the other hand the ale brewed in the monastery was sometimes 'so weak that the pigs would not drink of it' as the Archbishop said in 1515. Neither would the monks who, we are told, 'escaped' through The Porta Monachorum, the great gate onto the Market Place, to seek better ale. Later the Dean and Chapter brewed ale and small beer; verger William Southby, the last to carry on this tradition, brewed ale in part of the Porta until 1858. Many public houses had brewed their own ale but, by the mid-19th century, few did so and there were four main breweries: the Waterside Brewery, the Quay Brewery, Legge's in Newnham Street and the small Eagle Brewery in Cambridge Road. The Waterside Brewery in the 17th century belonged to Mr Marche and was purchased by the Hall family, who later transferred the business to the new Forehill Brewery of 1871, built near the site of the former Holy Trinity Workhouse. John Harlock then bought the Three Crowns, 'with a small brewery attached to it at The Quay' which he expanded. After earlier amalgamations A. & B. Hall Ltd and Cutlack and Harlock Ltd joined to become Hall, Cutlack and Harlock Ltd in 1930. Further changes eventually led to Watney Mann (East Anglia) Ltd becoming the owners in 1967. Two years later the last Ely brewery closed, but not before a celebration brew, called 'Bona Cervisia', recalling the best ale produced by Ely monks, marked St Etheldreda's day on 23 June 1968.

A great variety of goods made in Ely were produced on a small scale. The Bursar's accounts for 1526 refer to the making of '92 lbs. of wax into torches and lights 3s 10d' and the purchase of '10 lbs of candles 20d'. The dozen or so mediaeval guilds in Ely all appear to have existed to provide candles to burn in church, for masses to be said and for other observances on certain saints' days and occasionally to help members in need. For example, the brothers and sisters of one guild were to 'provide a wax taper weighing three quarters of a pound, to stand on the great altar, and to be lighted daily at the mass of the Blessed Virgin Mary' and at other times; 30 masses were to be said on the death of any member over 16. In this century there was at least one small factory near the present Witchford Road where tallow candles were made, and High Street Passage was known as Tallow Passage in the 18th century. There were a number of potteries and, at a factory the earliest part of which was built in 1836, leather was tanned and curried. Asparagus was still sent to London at the end of the 19th century when Thomas Pashlar, 'one of the enterprising gardeners' of Ely, on one occasion 'grew 500 asparagus heads, some 18 inches long and 3½ round'.

The early years of the present century saw the beginning of relatively larger manufacturing enterprises. By the First World War the currier's business of 1836 begun by Nathaniel Simpson, and carried on by the Blakeman family, had expanded to more than twice its original size; the number of employees was about one hundred. By the 1930s only three were employed and, with the death of Thomas Blakeman, fourth generation, the business and premises were sold in 1944. A mainly retail trade was carried on for over twenty-five years until the factory and nearby house were demolished in 1973 to make way for a four-storey office block, on the corner of Fore Hill and Broad Street.

'Granger's Fruit Preserving Company will, we may confidently expect, operate beneficially upon the neighbourhood. Besides the number of hands which must be employed, and the consequent money circulation, there is the profit arising to the place from a ready market being found for orchard and garden fruit, of which as a rule there is a large supply.' So a business opened in the previous year was welcomed in the *Ely Almanack* (1891), published by Ely printer William Creak. It flourished and new premises were erected in 1909 from which the company continued to trade into the early 1920s. From the mid-1930s to 1959 St Martin (Eastern) Ltd produced marmalade and jam and it is this company whose name is remembered in St Martin's Walk, a small housing development built in 1987. The factory was subsequently used by Dorman Sprayers and by Eastern Counties Printers, before it was demolished in 1986. Once it housed a 'Shopping Week' during 1936 when Ely traders displayed their wares to about 2,000 visitors; an unusual event at that time. Later Homes and Trades Exhibitions were held on Paradise Recreation Ground.

On the outskirts of the City at Queen Adelaide, the Beet Sugar Factory opened in October 1925 on an area formerly known as Turbutsey. The factory had its own railway sidings and a fleet of 50 barges and, with about 500 employees, the largest workforce in Ely. It closed after the 1980/1 season and is now used by G.G. Papworth Ltd, storage and distribution specialists.

Gradually, from the middle of the 19th century, Ely became an important railway junction and so a variety of railway workers lived in the City. 81 employees, from stationmaster to engine drivers and porters, covered the work at the station, in the office, on the line and on the trains. Railway Terrace, now Castelhithe, was built to house railway workers and there too was the GER Refreshment Room for ladies until at least 1893. The Eastern Dock, near the railway crossing, opened in 1846 and enabled coal to be transferred from train to barge and so delivered to the pumping stations. On the day the dock opened several people were heard to exclaim 'What will the quiet old city of Ely come to?' The reporter then suggested that, with the increase in trade, in commerce, cattle and general merchandise, the term 'Ely a Port' would soon be 'justly and properly applied'. The amount of trade, particularly on market days, certainly increased; a stream of people from surrounding villages made their way along Broad Street to the Market Place and this could still be seen only 50 years ago. The Ely Co-operative Society enlarged its premises in Broad Street in 1916 and the number of public houses on the route grew to at least 15 by the turn of the century; a new church was built. With the increase of motor transport, trade in this part of the City declined by the end of World War II, but more recently Broad Street has again become a trading area. This is partly due to the siting of two small factories which produced plastics and lampshades, on a site where once there had been a walled garden attached to brewer Harlock's Quayside house. Later Tesco Stores converted the larger of the two buildings into a supermarket, which opened for trading in 1982; it is now, with the exception of the King's School, the largest employer in the City, with over 230 employees.

In the 20 years after the 1939-45 war, 12 manufacturing firms were established, of which two have survived, but with different names and management. The long-standing Ely firm G. & J. Peck has been joined at Lisle Lane by two chemical factories, and two trading estates have opened – one on the former Witchford Road airfield, appropriately named Lancaster Way, is privately run, while the Cambridgeshire Business Park, run by the District Council, is sited at Angel Drove near the railway station.

In monastic times a market was held weekly, largely for local trade, on roughly the same site as today, though it may well have extended further to the west, perhaps into the area known now as Butcher's Row. Application was made to the 'Lord Bishop of Ely, Lord of the Royal Franchise of Ely' to alter market day from Saturday to Thursday. The application was approved and it has been held on that day since 1801. On the Market Place for many years, cattle, sheep and horses were sold as well as produce, and during the 19th century traders' stalls were set up in front of the Corn Exchange. 'The Ely Fairs and Cattle Market and Corn Exchange Company' had erected this building, which the *Cambridge Chronicle* of 20 March 1847 announced as 'entirely finished this week'. The nearby room on the Buttermarket side was converted in 1855 into a Public Reading Room.

The Cattle Market, behind the former White Hart, opened in November 1846 and traders' stalls, as perhaps in earlier days, then moved to the main part of the Market Place. Later, Unwin's sold ladders, sheds and small farm implements in front of the Corn Exchange. At the Cattle Market, Frank Grain and later George Comins auctioned cattle, sheep and pigs; Grain's held the last sale of this type in 1981. A variety of produce and goods was sold every Thursday by Comins, and from 1980 an auction of secondhand cars took place on Monday evenings. In the 1980s plans were discussed for a Shopping Development there, but by the beginning of 1990 no decision had been reached.

Fairs in Ely date back to the early days of the monastery; before 1135 an undated charter was granted by Henry I, which gave permission for a fair to be held for seven days at the Feast of St Etheldreda in June. So successful was this that it was suppressed for a time in the mid-13th century, as it was thought to be interfering with the profit of the Westminster Fair. By the end of the century it was not only flourishing but was extended to nine days. After this there were three fairs for a while but, by 1665, there was only that at the end of May and that of St Audrey (an alternative name for Etheldreda); Bishop Wren forbade the holding of both that year due to the Plague. St Audrey's Fair was later moved to the date of her translation, 17 October. At one time necklaces, known as St Audrey's lace, were sold at Ely and, by the 17th century, had become symbolic of the cheap and gaudy finery found at such fairs, giving to the language the word 'tawdry'.

The tradition of proclaiming the Fair, a ceremony now performed by the Mayor was, until the 1930s, carried out by the Bailiff who, accompanied by the Town Crier with his bell and preceded by a fiddler, read the charter at Parnell Pits, St John's Road where a stock fair was held, on St Mary's Green for the horse fair, at the Market Place 'for the merry-making' and at Waterside for the cheese fair. In 1913, on a day when the weather was glorious, the villagers streamed in from the surrounding district and St Mary's Street was 'alive with cows, heifers, and calves . . . horses were paraded up and down for the inspection of would be purchasers'. The horse fair gradually died out and today the only fair is that held twice yearly at the end of May and October to provide entertainment and fun. As it is on Thursday, Friday and Saturday, the market traders are ousted from their usual position on the first day and moved to cramped quarters along the north side of High Street.

LEFT: P.F. Tow had his shop at the western end of the Buttermarket until c1925. He advertised as 'fish and ice merchant & game dealer; fish in season fresh every day; established 1858'. The large sturgeon was caught about six miles from Ely. ABOVE: Bringing in osiers or rushes c1900, both of which were grown near Ely. BELOW: stripping the willow.

ABOVE: Landing osiers at Fear's Rod Yard at the river end of the Three Blackbirds yard. LEFT: Sam Cox sits at work on a basketmaker's plank in Fear's Basket Works at Waterside c1920. The bottomless baskets stacked on the right were each placed in the neck of a sack to act as a funnel and so facilitate the loading of potatoes. RIGHT: Paul Gotobed, in his back yard near Lisle Lane, is making an eel trap; it is smaller than the eel grigs which stand at the side.

ABOVE: Cutting asparagus spears early in the 20th century at W.B. Granger's asparagus beds in The Vineyards. BELOW: The Forehill Brewery shortly before its demolition pre-1973; Jones' sweet shop (on left) and the Glazier's Arms have gone but the brewery gateposts remain. OPPOSITE ABOVE: Quay Brewery c1929; during World War II, cellars here were used as an Air Raid Shelter. (CC) BELOW: This photo c1900 by John Titterton was taken from the top of the brewery chimney. (BL and MW)

67

RIGHT: This ruined building (once to the north of Witchford Road) is the remains of a tallow candle factory. ABOVE: Blakeman's Leather Factory, part of which dates from at least 1836; the wooden louvres opened so that the treated leather could be dried. This photo was taken shortly before demolition, 1973. BELOW: The Ely 'Jam' Factory in the course of erection, 1890. OPPOSITE ABOVE: The construction of the Beet Sugar Factory at Turbutsey, near Queen Adelaide, 1925. CENTRE: The Market Place (1845) before the Sessions House was demolished; beyond (right) is the building on the corner of High Street, once The Dolphin public house. BELOW: A group of citizens enjoy a view of the Market c1955. On the left is ex-police sergeant Moll, on the right Harry S. Speller.

ABOVE LEFT: The Dolphin. RIGHT: Trade tokens were issued during the 17th century by publicans and tradesmen as small change; one was from Thomas Chadrton at the White Swan on the Market Place. BELOW LEFT: Part of a typical Thursday market c1970. RIGHT: 19th century billheads; Joshua Taylor later moved to Cambridge, where this well-known firm continues to trade. BELOW: The Bell Hotel 1853; the ground floor is now occupied by Savory & Moore, Chemists.

ABOVE: The Horse Fair outside St Mary's Church, 1845. (CC) BELOW: The County Agricultural Show (1887) was held in Ely; this arch linked the Angel and King Charles in the Oak along Station Road.

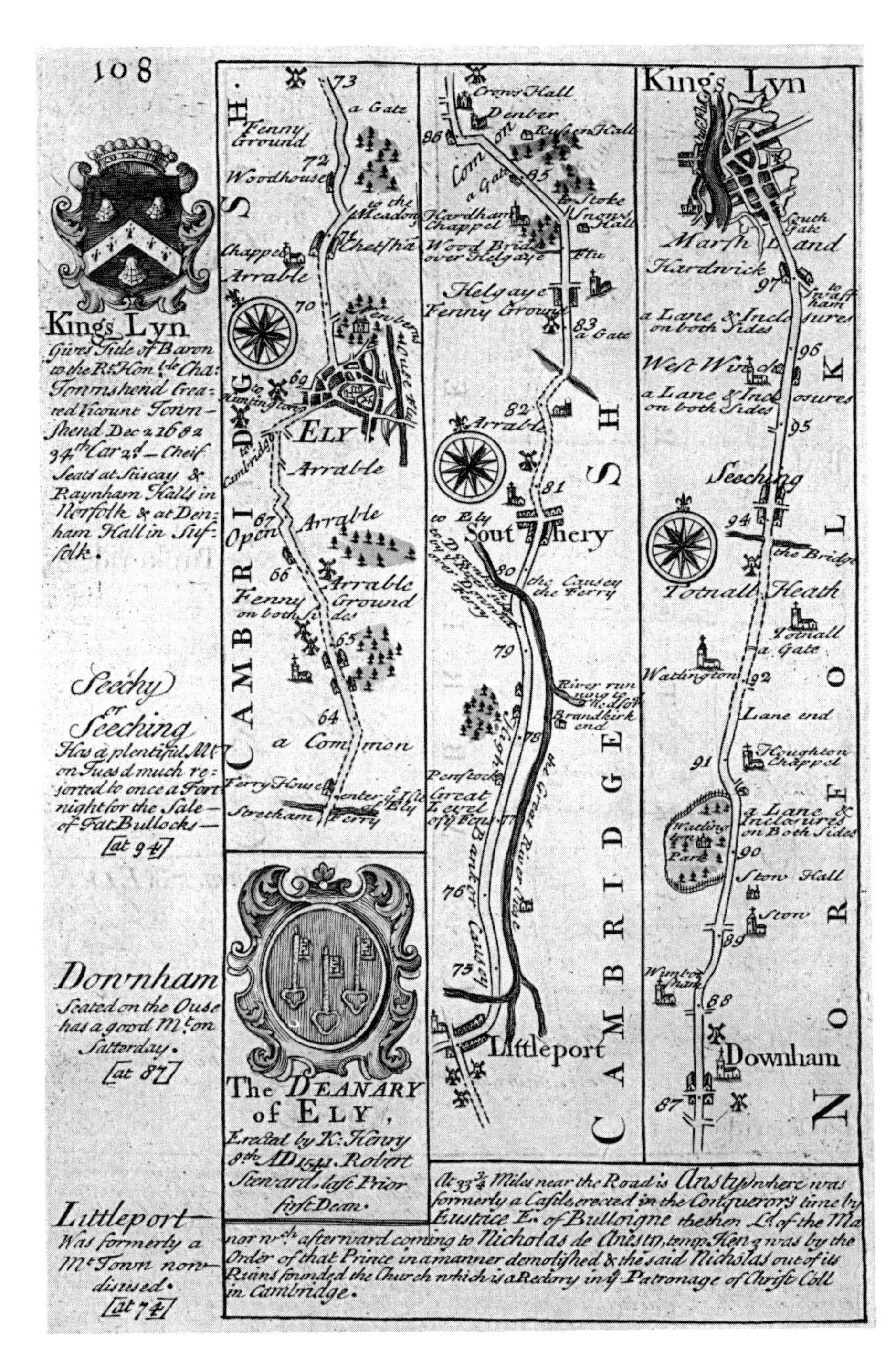

Detail from a 17th century map based on Ogilby's; note the coat of arms of the Dean and Chapter.

Along the Way

For centuries Ely was set apart and in many ways unfashionably behind the times, but not as isolated as many imagine. Even before the Conquest, in the early days of the monastery, travellers came to the City, and indeed St Etheldreda herself journeyed to Northumberland and later home from Coldingham. There is considerable evidence of communication between monastic settlements; the job of the Hostiller at the monastery was to receive 'strangers and travellers . . .'. E.R. Chapman tells us in his *Notes on the Sacrist Rolls of Ely* (1907) that the reception and accommodation provided at the monastery varied 'according to their degrees'. Although there is no need to look further than the considerable bulk of the Cathedral for evidence that people and goods travelled to Ely, the Sacrist Rolls provide much information; in the earliest it appears that the then Bishop, de Luda, visited London, Balsham and Norwich in 1290. Purchases were made from the fairs at Bury, Barnwell, Boston and Reach and from the port of Lynn, and London was visited for payment of tax arrears. The Precentor went to Balsham in 1361 'to enquire for books' and the Bishop journeyed to and from his various residences.

Many of these early journeys must have been partly or entirely along the waterways and in the winter months travelling through the fenland could only have been a cold and hazardous undertaking. This is confirmed by the story already told of King Canute's visit across 'the bending and cracking ice' when 'after a few falls . . . they all got safe to Ely' along the Stuntney causeway. For centuries the waterways provided the only possible year-round route for people and goods to and from Ely though, when passable, rough dirt tracks, sometimes known as corduroy roads, were also used by travellers on foot and on horseback. Today pleasure boats form the majority of craft on the Ouse; a string of barges, drawn no longer by a horse but by a power boat, is an unusual sight. Pigot's *Directory* (1823) noted 'WATER CONVEYANCE. CAMBRIDGE, Lynn, Bury, and places intervening & adjacent, occasionally; John Cross, Sen., Richard Hawkes, Abraham Johnson, William Laws, John Lee, & Thomas Smith'.

The year 1830 saw the opening of the South Level Cut which, shorter than the former winding route *via* Prickwillow, forms a direct route by river between Ely and Littleport; it also effectively drains an area of 'sedgy moors' at Padnal and Waterden. The occasion was marked by a procession of decorated barges headed by that of the Commissioners. Celebrations ended with an 'excellent dinner' at the Lamb, 'served up in a style reflecting the highest credit on the landlord, William Beecroft'. William Harrison, 'Poet Laureate of the Fens', wrote a poem to mark the event, from which the following lines are quoted:

'Hope with grateful eye surveys
Bright anticipated days
When the swain shall plough and sow
Where the fisher used to row:
Waving cornfields supersede
Swampy wastes of sedge and reed:
Bleating sheep and lowing kine
In the future concert join
Where the bittern's hollow boom
Echo'd through the dreary gloom.'

The two-mile long Stuntney causeway is of great importance and perhaps dates to the Bronze Age. In the 14th century, repairs were carried out annually with money provided by the church at Wentworth; this belonged to the Prior and convent. Later, repairs became the responsibility of the Dean and Chapter, for example £20 was allocated for 'mending Highways' in 1541. John Ogilby's maps of c1675 show that many roads (tracks by today's standards) were in use, including two going through Ely: one from London to King's Lynn, the other from Huntingdon to Ipswich. The first passed through Cambridge to Ely *via* Stretham and to Lynn through Chettisham and Littleport, the second through St Ives, Sutton, Ely, Stuntney, Soham and Bury *en route* to Ipswich. The country was covered with a network of these tracks, many starting from London, which provided not only for travellers on foot and horseback but also for those in wheeled vehicles, although we are told they did not supersede 'the old channels of communication with which the inhabitants of the fen districts were most familiar' for many centuries.

When Celia Fiennes visited Ely in 1698, side-saddle on horseback, she came from the direction of Stuntney and passed 'a flatt on a gravel Causey' from which 'Ely looked finely' through the trees. 'In winter this Causey is over flowed and they have no way but boates to pass in . . .'. Within the City she said that pavement 'would make it look more properly an habitation for human beings . . .'. Celia's fenland journey of 1698 was repeated by Alison Payne on her horse, Mighty. When they visited Ely on 21 June 1988 they found a City of 'tidy streets and well-kept houses' and in the Cathedral 'so heavenly was the singing, so uplifting the beautiful architecture' that the demands of the journey were forgotten.

The early 18th century saw improvement in many roads but the first Turnpike Trust was not established in Ely until 1763. This led to work earlier advocated by Canon James Bentham, the great 18th century historian of Ely's Cathedral and monastery. The route to Cambridge from Soham *via* Ely ceased to follow the present St John's Road, to leave Ely by Bugg's Hill, as Cambridge Road was then called. Much material for this road was obtained from the field known as 'Hilly Pieces', near the former Barton Farm. After 1764 travellers crossed the River Ouse on their way to Cambridge by a new bridge at Stretham, instead of by ferry. The construction of other Turnpike roads followed and a surveyor sent by J.L. McAdam was appointed in 1822 to 'take the Management of all the Roads in the Neighbourhood at the Salary of 2gns a week he finding himself a Horse'. Gates at Ely, where money was collected for the upkeep of the roads, were at Bugg's Hill and the Stone Bridge (perhaps the High Bridge, then of stone). It was planned that toll-houses should be built or bought and perhaps a small house in St Mary's Street, known as Weighbridge Cottage, was used as a toll-house for many years; here the weighbridge could still be seen until about 1970. Since World War II the Turnpike posts made in 1852 by Wilkinson's, whose foundry was on the corner of Chapel

Street and Downham Road, have been returned to near their original positions on the roads to Cambridge, Witchford, Lynn and Stuntney. After the Cambridge and Ely Roads Act 1852, roads on the Ely side of each post became the responsibility of the City of Ely Local Board of Health.

Pigot & Co's *Directory* (1823) notes that carriers left Ely for destinations between Lynn and London at the rate of almost one a day, except at weekends, though transport to Littleport provided by Thos Browning was available every evening at five from the Bell. Newmarket was only served by the carrier on Thursday, Sutton and Soham two and three times weekly. *The Royal Mail* coach travelled to Cambridge from the Red Lion every evening at five and every weekday either *Nelson's* or *The Union* coach could be taken at 11.00 am.

In the 19th century the road to Stuntney continued to cause difficulties; the local press cautioned that 'the materials of this turnpike road between Ely and Soham are now worn down to the black moor, and there are some dangerous ruts and holes'. Even in the present century this road has needed regular attention. Now the Stuntney by-pass slightly to the east, completed in December 1986, has made use of new technology, which should ensure a long-lasting surface. The other ancient 'way in' to the Isle along the Aldreth causeway is only a drove or track today.

Many of the small tracks in the nearby fen remained as corduroy roads, unpassable by motor vehicles until the Second World War, when most were concreted. A rhythmic bumping can still be felt by car travellers, as the wheels cross the joins between the lengths of concrete now hidden under tarmacadam. Typical of these roads is that which links Ely directly to the village of Coveney; predictably it has been widened beyond the concrete and so the sides often crack and break away in a characteristic manner.

The bridges near Ely needed much attention and for a time this was the responsibility of the Bishop. The building of the first stone bridge between Ely and Stuntney is recorded in the Sacrist Roll of the 14th century but where this crossed the river is not certain. Baskerville, who travelled to Ely in 1681, was alarmed by the bridges in the area, even after a dry winter — 'the rotten bridges with our horses, being glad to alight for fear they should break through and stick in the rotten bogs under them'. An inconvenient three or four span wooden bridge was replaced by a 'new and handsome bridge' of stone in 1833. Twenty years later the Ely Bridge Committee made application to the Dean and Chapter for 'assistance in improving the Ely bridge'. On the site of the 1833 bridge a concrete three span one was constructed in 1981 to replace a 1909 iron structure, which had been built a little to the south. Of the three other bridges which cross the Ouse near Ely today, two are railway bridges. The third, built in the 1960s, is a simple concrete structure giving access to the marina area now occupying Babylon.

The railway reached the City when the Eastern Counties line from Newport, Essex to Brandon was constructed in 1845 *via* Cambridge and Ely; this line linked the Norfolk Railway to Norwich. Both lines were opened on 29 July, when the band of the Coldstream Guards travelled from Shoreditch to play at Ely. There dignitaries from Norwich and Norfolk were received by a guard of honour and visited the Cathedral before continuing to Cambridge for further celebrations. The station, at first a temporary wooden structure, was approached by a curved road sweeping up to the entrance. Only remnants of the more permanent 1847 building survive but improvements to it and to the approach were begun in 1989. In spite of the 'most hazardous undertaking' of the construction of railways across the fens, by the end of the century lines were opened from Ely to King's Lynn, March and Peterborough, to Newmarket and Bury St Edmunds and on to Harwich, also to nearby Sutton (later extended to St Ives). Of these only the latter has been closed and the rails removed; another change is that the passenger route to Newmarket from Ely is now *via* Cambridge. The first railway bridge, built 1844/5, to carry trains of the Eastern Counties Railway over the river slightly to the north-east of the High Bridge, crossed the river for the second time, a short distance to the north. The latter bridge has the curious name of Common Muckill, known by local people as Carmuckill. The former, originally of wood, was replaced in 1896 by a 'new wrought-iron bridge of one span, of some 300 tons dead weight and 130 feet long'. Its erection was considered a 'Smart Engineering Feat' carried out as it was during the early hours of a 'wild, wet and stormy' November Sunday morning, in order that the Great Eastern Railway line between London and Norwich should be closed for the minimum time. It was confirmed in 1989 that the London line from Cambridge to Lynn is to be electrified.

The railway opened up new possibilities for surrounding villagers, many of whom could then reach Ely easily and quickly though, from the late 19th century description by A.D. Bayne, Ely was not a desirable place to visit, 'an amphibious-looking place – houses, meadows and water strangely intermingled, and masked and fringed by willows.' Even in the 1970s, residents from such isolated villages as Hockwold came to Ely by train to shop at the market.

The accompanying extract reprinted from Pigot & Co's *Directory* (1830) gives full information about available transport at that time. *The City of Ely Red Book* (1920) says nothing about transport by rail (not an indication that this means of travel had ceased) but lists ten 'Carriers to and from Ely' who left from the Chequers, the Club Inn, the Dolphin, White Hart, Lamb Tap, King's Arms and Blake's shop (probably in Broad Street) for villages within a ten mile radius.

COACHES.

To LONDON, the *Union* (from Lynn) calls at the Bell Inn, every Tuesday, Thursday, and Saturday morning at eleven, and at the Lamb, every Monday, Wednesday, and Friday at the same hour; goes through Cambridge, Barkway, and Ware.

To CAMBRIDGE, the *Telegraph*, from the Lamb and Bell Inns, every Tuesday, Thursday, and Saturday morning at eight—the same *Coach* (from Upwell) calls at the Lamb and Bell Inns, every Monday, Wednesday, & Friday morning at eight—and William Crabb's *Sociable*, from his own house, every Monday, Wednesday, Thursday, and Saturday morning at seven.

To LYNN, the *Union* (from London) calls at the Bell Inn, every Monday, Wednesday, and Friday afternoon at four, and at the Lamb Inn, every Tuesday, Thursday, and Saturday at the same hour; goes thro' Littleport and Downham Market.

To UPWELL, the *Telegraph* (from Cambridge) calls at the Lamb and Bell Inns, every Tues. Thurs. & Sat. evening at 7.

CARRIERS.

To LONDON, Marsh & Swann's *Fly Vans*, from the Dolphin, every morning (Sunday excepted) at seven; their *Waggons*, every Monday and Thursday afternoon at two—and Isaac Benton's *Waggon*, from the Black Swan, every Thursday morning.

To LITTLEPORT, Robert Thornhill's *Cart*, from the Club Inn, every afternoon (Sunday excepted.)

To LYNN, Marsh & Swann's *Fly Vans*, from the Dolphin, every forenoon (Sunday excepted) at eleven.

To MEPAL, Joseph Bell's *Cart*, from the Red Lion. every Thursday afternoon.

To NEWMARKET, Thomas Smith's *Cart*, from the Club Inn, every Thursday afternoon.

To SOHAM, Robert Ower's *Cart*, from the Club Inn, every Monday & Thursday afternoon.

To WISBEACH, John Beagly's *Cart*, from the Club Inn, every Thurs. afternoon.

CONVEYANCE BY WATER.

To CAMBRIDGE, Marsh and Swann's *Boats*, every Monday night, and to LYNN, every Saturday night.

To CAMBRIDGE, LYNN, NORTHAMPTON, BURY ST. EDMUNDS, BECKFORD, HUNTINGDON, and all intermediate places, Abraham Johnson's, William Law's, and Thomas Smith's *Lighters*, occasionally.

By 1989 *The City of Ely Official Guide* stated that 'Ely is a major railway junction served by express trains to Cambridge and London (Liverpool Street). There are also regular services to Littleport, Downham Market and King's Lynn; to March and Peterborough; to Thetford, Wymondham and Norwich; to Bury St Edmunds and Ipswich; to Peterborough, Stamford, Leicester and Birmingham and to Doncaster'. Road transport is mentioned; Cambus provide local services to Cambridge, Newmarket and St Ives with some additional ones on Thursdays. Another firm operates a service to March on weekdays but the only Sunday service is to Cambridge. No 'express' service now comes through Ely and 'bus services in general have been much reduced in the years since World War II. In 1989 there began 'The Ely Tour', which took passengers around Ely on an open-top double-decker 'bus, with a commentary on the City.

The nearest airport is at Cambridge. The only aircraft to land in Ely recently, apart from the RAF 'plane which crashed about 100 metres from the Cathedral in 1951, are helicopters. These occasionally land on school playing-fields, but more often at the Royal Air Force Hospital, usually to bring patients or important visitors. The Princess of Wales visited the Hospital on 9 July 1987, when she was received by station commander Group Captain John Baird; the hospital was then renamed the Princess of Wales RAF Hospital, Ely. She toured the hospital before opening the Cathedral Festival of Flowers.

Communications in other ways have followed national patterns. Letters carried by travellers in monastic times went later by mail cart. There may have been a 'post office of some sort' in the 17th century and by 1823, according to Pigot's *Directory*, Robert Edwards was Post Master in the High Street; this was still so in 1839. Then mail arrived about 9.00 am and left for Cambridge at 6.00 pm. The cost varied according to distance until the advent of the Penny Post, whereupon thousands of letters were received weekly in Ely compared with about 300 previously. By 1847 John Clements was Post Master in premises at the Market Place. He revealed the curious postal addresses given to Ely as 'Oil of eeley, pile of heley, highle of Eligh'. The chief Post Office was on the corner of Minster Place in 1884 and it was about ten years before it moved to Market Street. Here it stayed, although rebuilt in 1891, until the present office opened in 1966. There were once sub-post offices at Jefferson's in St Mary's Street opposite St Mary's Church, at Aveling's in Broad Street, then on the opposite side of the road, and later at the Tuck Shop in Station Road. The only one to remain is in St John's Stores on the corner of St John's Road and West End.

In January 1905 the *Ely Weekly Guardian* noted 'Ely during the past few months witnessed the introduction of the telephone which has greatly benefited the principal business men of the city'. Among the first were Cole Ambrose of Stuntney (number one), Harold Archer, solicitor (three), the Lamb Hotel (four) and Barclays Bank (five). The first public 'phone box was not installed until 1923; at least one familiar red box is to remain on Barton Square, though all others will gradually be changed to the new, more anonymous, type. Cellnet established a link on the Cathedral west tower in 1987 and Fax, one of the most modern links, is available at several places in the city.

In 1973, after a gap of some years, a Town Crier again appeared briefly on Ely's streets and occasionally since then a volunteer crier has appeared in costume. They followed the tradition of 18th century John Langford, 19th century John Harle and John Toombs and, in this century for about 25 years, blind Read Wayman, followed by James Ankin.

A different type of link, that of friendship and cultural exchange, was formed in 1956 with the Danish town of Ribe, and East Cambridgeshire District is twinned with Orsay in France and Kempen in Germany.

The heading from Sacrist Roll VIII 1339/1340 which refers to Alan of Walsingham Sacrist of Ely. It was written on parchment. (ULC)

ABOVE: Ely from the river c1850; this watercolour by an unknown artist shows the first railway bridge and (left) a small building near the High Bridge, which may be a toll house. (CC) CENTRE: The Lamb Corner, a print published 1848, shows (right) the milestone which stood on the corner near the present Lloyds Bank until it was demolished by a lorry in the early 1930s. From a position in about the middle of the picture Ely's traffic was directed by a RAC man during the 1930s. BELOW: Ely High Bridge, 1833.

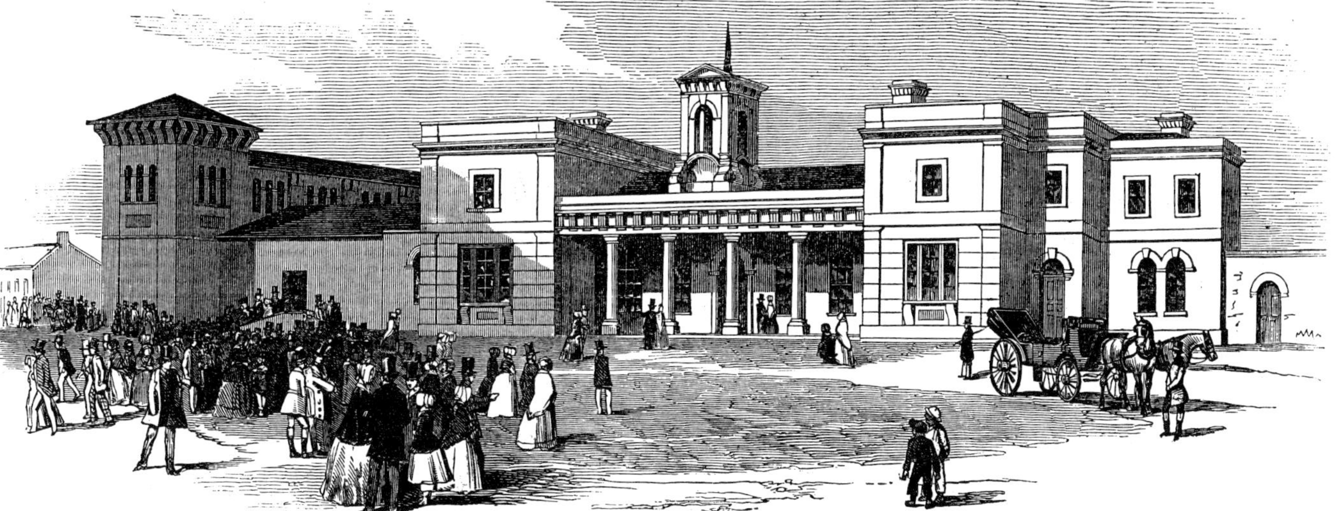

ABOVE: Alex Findley & Co of Motherwell constructed this Ely High Bridge in 1909; it was opened in 1910. CENTRE: Ely Railway Station from an engraving published in *The Illustrated London News* 30 October 1847; 'an extensive pile in pleasing mixed Grecian and Italian style'. BELOW: Beyond 'Carmuckill' Bridge to the north-east lies Cuckoo Bridge. This John Titterton watercolour of 1899 shows the picturesque brick bridge destroyed c1940 to allow larger boats to enter the Roswell Pits from the river. The track across the bridge led in mediaeval times from Ely to Turbutsey.

ABOVE: This view from the railway crossing near the station and shows the Crown Inn, partly hidden by the coach. BELOW The view from the front of the station before small industry was developed in the area c1850. Almost in the centre is the Ange Inn.

LEFT: Town Crier 'Blind Wayman' proclaiming Ely Fair in 1908. (CC) RIGHT: Queen Mary, then the Queen Mother, and the present Queen Mother when she was Queen, visit Ely 21 January 1938. BELOW: A post card c1912 which shows the approach to the City centre, when there were garages to right and left and Brand's blacksmiths shop (near the horseless carriage).

ABOVE: Miss Ethel Drake, in her Ford car c1915, was almost certainly the only woman in Ely to have a driving licence, when she first helped her father run the family taxi firm from their home at Railway Terrace. Her longest trip was to Norwich and back, at 25 mph. LEFT: The White Hart; a billhead dated 1829, when it cost 5s to hire a room for a meeting. RIGHT: Outside Cutlack's, which faced onto High Street; the bank was on the corner of Chequer Lane until c1923. BELOW: The Lamb Hotel in 1853.

The Poor, the Sick & the Prisoners

The Poor

Charity in Ely almost certainly began at the monastery and would have been distributed through the Elemosinarius or Almoner from the Almonry on the north side of the monastery facing the Market Square. Although the Almoner had considerable means at his disposal and presented annual accounts to the Chapter of moneys dispersed, scraps of meat and bread were also distributed. The Sacrist Rolls of 1339-40 record £3 given at various times to the poor of Ely and elsewhere. Many of the bishops also gave to the poor; for example Bishop West gave meat and drink to 200 at his gate daily and also 'many occasional largesses'. The guilds too gave some relief as emergencies arose, to the needy of the 14th century and later.

At the Dissolution this assistance came to an end, though £20 was allowed to be 'distributed yerely in Almes'. By the end of the 16th century much of the Almoner's function was taken over by the Parish Officers; poor relief to people unable to support themselves was a matter for individual parishes. Churchwardens and overseers of the poor, elected annually, levied a rate on householders which was spent to help the aged, disabled, feeble-minded, orphans, abandoned children, unemployed and other needy people.

Later many charities grew up to supplement this relief though at least one, founded by Thomas Parson, was established earlier, in the mid-15th century. Little is known of Thomas Parson, though it is probable that his family had been in Ely from the beginning of the century or earlier and that land at Stretham was bequeathed by him to the charity. As funds increased, property was bought: Shinkwyns on Babylon and Chamber's Holt nearby, both alder grounds, also the Red House on the site of the present English College in Waterside. By 1622, after a tax which had benefited the Sovereign fell into disuse, the revenue of the charity had so accumulated that a charter was obtained to establish Feoffees, 'The Governors of the Lands and Possessions of the Poor in Ely', charged to relieve poverty and sickness. Parson's Charity once owned a house in Broad Street known as Friton's or Fritten's, and is noted on one of two Benefactions Boards, above the door leading from the Lady Chapel into the north transept of the Cathedral. The property was given by Mr Friton and Mr Cockain as 'a lott & several Tenemts to widows paying 6s 8d per annum rent' and was abandoned after new Parson's Charity almshouses were built in 1844 by architect George Basevi in St Mary's Street, 'a better quarter of the city'. Earlier in the 17th century, the Governors leased Dr Hitch's house on the corner of Silver Street and The Gallery and, we are told, made good use of it until 1696; it was part school, part bridewell and part workhouse. The charity bought the house in the Palace Green c1660, next to the present-day library, from Robert Claxton, cathedral organist. He continued to live there for some time but by 1665 the poor and needy were housed with Elizabeth Bracher in charge, until it was sold c1708.

Individuals who hoped to benefit had to submit a petition backed by one or more of the Feoffees. William Balaam pursued his claim for some years; he had cut his leg badly in 1667 and asked for 'money to pay a skilful surgeon' lest he be in danger 'to have his leg cutt off'. He continued to petition until his death in 1673. John Lame, fisherman 'much vissitted with a great and tedious sicknes, Soe that hee is therby utterly ruined and undone' said that 'if some Speedy and charrittable worke bee not wrought upon him, hee of necessity is like to bee starved for wante of present sustinence to preserve life'. It was recommended that he be given 10s. Another petitioner was not so favourably treated in spite of, or perhaps because of, the way she described herself as 'poore weake feeble sorrie miserable fullorne despised disdained distressed and forever undone . . .'. Clothing was provided for poor children and in the 19th century £500 was given towards the building of the National Schools. Relief in kind was given for various reasons, as when there was a shortage of corn at the beginning of the 19th century; a quarter of the weekly allowance was given as rice. Well-to-do citizens such as Thomas Page also occasionally gave in kind; 'a bullock weighing near 60 stone, together with 100 loaves of bread to the poor . . . which was a comfortable relief to them'.

Money continued to be regularly distributed to the needy of both Ely parishes and from 1865 coals, clothing and money to some, to others coals only. This arrangement ceased in about 1955 but people in need are still helped and money is deposited with the Department of Social Security during cold weather to help meet bills for extra heating.

Many Parson's Charity governors signed their names at the foot of documents by the mid-17th century. Luke Dench, lawyer, Thomas Page of Bedford House, Jonathan Page and other prominent citizens signed as governors, but undoubtedly the only one known nationally was Oliver Cromwell. Other signatories included William Wagstaffe, a Governor of Parson's Charity for about 20 years and one who issued trade tokens bearing the arms of the Worshipful Company of Fishmongers, and William Turkinton, who was churchwarden of Holy Trinity and mace bearer for the Bedford Level Corporation, who also issued tokens, but as a candlemaker. William Gotobed, however, only made his mark. His surname, which frequently occurs in the history of Ely, is said to mean 'bright one of God', though there are other interpretations.

The funds of the Ely Dispensary were transferred in 1953 to Parson's Charity. Today it owns the Parson's Square Almshouses, four modern, double almshouses in Deacon's Lane, which replaced four on the south side of Waterside in use until the mid-1960s, three other small houses, over 800 acres of land in the fen area and Bamford House, Deacon's Lane, opened in 1976. This house is named after Dr Brian Bamford, a much-loved and respected doctor, who came to Ely in 1934 and, apart from war service, practised until he retired in 1972.

The second of the large charities still operating is that set up after the will of Catherine Needham, widow of Rev Needham of Ely. Among her possessions was the White Hart Inn 'with cherry ground thereto belonging', 18 acres of fen and a house in Newnham Street. About ten years after her death the school and schoolmaster's house provided for in her will were built in 1740 on Back Hill, and money provided for boys' education and clothing. There is no longer a Needham's School in Ely but the four-storey block on the Downham Road campus is known as 'Needham's' so that the charity can continue to function for the benefit of education in the City.

Many Ely charities are listed on the Benefactions Boards, including Parson's and Needham's, but most are small and a majority incorporated into the two larger ones towards the end of the last century. Among these were those of Anne Bell, Dr Turner, Lady Norton, Thomas Edghee, Samuel and William Cole, David Offley, Elizabeth Morley and Ann Bull. Money was also left to benefit Ely citizens by Margaret Walden, John Howard, Mary Austin, Robert Walden, John Usher, Gotobed East and Thomas Watkins. The latter gave £53 10d 2d to be invested; at first the interest was distributed to the poor in 6d amounts but later it was given in half crowns to the industrious poor 'as a more advisable mode of distribution'. And Gotobed East, a governor of Parson's Charity from 1729 to about 1753, gave tenements in Newnham Street for the use of poor widows. Still in existence as separate entities are Bishop Laney's Charity and Trinity Dole Charity. The former is shared with nearby Soham and awards grants for educational purposes. Trinity Dole gives small sums of money to help the poor and needy and, under its terms, the Vicar of Ely annually preaches a sermon for a fee of £2.

In Ely there have been at least five poorhouses. One was in part of a building on the site of Old Hereward Hall on the corner of Silver Street and The Gallery, and another in the Palace Green. St Mary's Workhouse, on the corner of Cambridge Road near the entrance to St Mary's Court was probably in course of construction in 1725. Later on this site stood the Plough and Fleece, which closed in 1932 almost 100 years after it opened. It was followed by the Kumin Café – advertised by a giant teapot outside – that was demolished in 1962. Trinity Workhouse, opened 1738 or earlier, stood near the bottom of Fore Hill, almost opposite the turn into Broad Street. This building only belonged to the Parish after William Cawthorne sold it about 1750. During the 1832 outbreak of cholera it was decided to use both workhouses for patients, after moving healthy inhabitants elsewhere; those from St Mary's went to William Raynor's house while Rev E.B. Sparke was requested to accommodate those from Holy Trinity Parish in part of the Almonry.

The Poor Law Amendment Act 1834 followed a period of low employment and inadequate wages. In Ely meetings were held, committees formed and the new Poor Law Union was created but St Mary's Workhouse continued to be used. The decision to build a new workhouse was taken in 1836 and the following year the Ely Union Workhouse to accommodate 340 was erected to the west of Cambridge Road, to serve both Ely parishes and a number of nearby villages. Workhouses usually accommodated paupers and, in the middle of the 19th century, when farmers could not afford to pay workers because of low corn prices, the workers declared that they would 'die by the roadside before this place [the workhouse] should hold them'. The Ely Benevolent Society, set up in 1851 to provide relief for those temporarily in need and not receiving parish relief, was administered to promote 'habits of industry and frugality . . .'. Today, much extended and improved, 'The Union' is a geriatric hospital and day centre known as Tower Hospital. Nearby an Isolation Hospital was opened in 1917 and continues as an annexe to the main building. The money raised on Hospital Sunday, as it has been known in Ely for many years, now benefits the Tower Hospital. Incidentally, Jonathan Page donated £500 to Addenbrooke's in 1840 and a group known as the 'Strolling Saints', based at the Highflyer public house, raised money for the hospital in the 1920s and '30s.

The Haven on Quayside, more recently Roglee, housed a laundry run by the Diocesan authorities and provided a home for unmarried mothers. It probably opened before 1913 and local people remember the women, dressed in grey, walking to St Peter's Church on Sundays. The Haven, which had done 'such a beneficient work among girls and young women', closed in 1937 and since then has been a private house.

The Sick

Provision for the sick goes back to the monastery; built soon after the Conquest, the monastic infirmary is now incorporated into buildings on either side of Firmary Lane to the south of the Cathedral. Powcher's Hall was used as the blood-letting house. Here for two or three days after the, as they thought, healthy practice of having blood taken, the monks were allowed to sleep in more comfortable quarters, have better food than was to be had in the main part of the monastery, and to use the private chapel. Rev D.J. Stewart reminds us that the 'Fermerye of a priory was not intended for sick monks only, but also for those who were infirm, or even refractory', but little is known of the Infirmarian himself since only one of his account rolls exists. Presumably, as the monastery offered assistance to the poor so, through the Almonry, it would have helped the sick outside its walls until the Dissolution, when others took responsibility. For example, Thomas Parson's gave to the sick as well as to the poor and, at a Holy Trinity vestry meeting of 1795, it was ordered that a salary of £20 per annum be allowed 'for medical Assistance to the poor of this parish including all cases of Medicine and Surgery' and a further guinea for every case of midwifery 'wherein the Assistance of a Surgeon is required' was agreed.

As with other cities, Ely was visited by the plague. In the 14th century the monk John of Wisbech, who had directed the building of the Lady Chapel, died of the plague or Black Death. There is reference in a document dated 1625 to 'the year when the plauge was in Ely' and there was smallpox 'in the town' when the burials at Holy Trinity were noted as 'exceptionally numerous'. The story of the well documented 1832 cholera outbreak has been told in Reg Holmes' *That Alarming Malady* (1974); this outbreak was followed four years later by one of influenza. Conditions were such that many suffered from various feverish conditions, often known as ague, and from scrofula (glandular swelling). There was a 'large use of narcotics' which 'pernicious habit increases death at all ages'. The inhabitants endeavoured to forget their external circumstances 'in the temporary excitement of these noxious drugs' which were laudanum, opium or a concoction called 'Godfrey's cordial'. It was said that 'the sale of laudanum in Ely was as common as the sale of butter and cheese . . .'

'Poppy tea and opium pill
Are the cure for many a fen ill'

and if neither worked, spiders could be tried, either swallowed or hung round the neck.

Conditions gradually improved and help increased. The Militia, stationed at Ely, built a small hospital used by them for about 30 years. The Ely Dispensary, built on land presented to the City, was opened in 1865 for the use of the parishioners of both parishes. Funded partly from central funds and partly by a small grant from Parson's Charity, free consultation and free medicine could be obtained by those who showed they could not pay; the poor 'reaped untold benefit . . .'. Soon after the turn of the century the Ely District Nursing Association (founded in 1886) later the Ely and District Nursing Trust, had its headquarters there. Well served from 1907-1939 by Nurse Clarke, a much respected and dedicated lady who, during her last year of service, was said to have paid 5,202 visits to the sick in Ely. The Dispensary was sold but continued as a clinic after the National Health Service started, and functioned as a pre-natal clinic until 1970 when the Health Centre in Chapel Street opened. Since then the Dispensary interior has been modernised and the building continues as a Day Centre for the elderly. Opened in the mid-1950s St Mary's Lodge takes in those who can no longer cope in their own homes; it is greatly helped by its 'Friends'. From 1970 the City has been served by a group of doctors, backed by a team of nurses and health workers, and by the Princess of Wales RAF Hospital which, since the 1950s, has admitted Ely citizens as patients.

Late in 1940 the former Bishop's Palace became a British Red Cross and St John's convalescent home for service-men as the former Theological College on Barton Square and the Grange had been during World War I. After the war, a school for physically handicapped children aged 5-16 opened in 1946 and remained for about 37 years. The children were noted for their wheelchair dancing and won a National Championship at the first attempt. The Sue Ryder Organisation then took over the lease and the first patient at this nursing home for the sick and disabled was admitted on 1 September 1986. The staff, assisted by volunteers, care devotedly for patients whose numbers will increase, it is hoped to 50, as the building is restored.

The Prisoners

It is difficult to be certain of the number and situation of every prison, bridewell or House of Correction which once existed in Ely, but the earliest recorded, the Prior's Prison, is that referred to in an inquisition taken in the 13th century. It was possibly on the northern side of the Porta or, before the end of the 14th century, when The Porta was built, in an earlier building. By the 17th century it was on the south, as suggested by the grafitti once there: 'John Hart Imprisoned here in the cause of the Gospel 1666'. The Bishop's Prison on Lynn Road is referred to in various documents from the late 13th century and, because it had become insecure, was partly rebuilt by Bishop Mawson in 1768. Continued lack of security also led, according to John Howard's report c1777, to the practice of securing prisoners by 'chaining them down on their backs upon a floor'. By 1810 this prison was much improved and continued until 1837, when the Bishop's jurisdiction ceased.

A bridewell, the City prison, mentioned by both Howard and James Neild (1812 report), was close by. Neild says it was built in 1651 and that a courtyard which it lacked could have been made in the 'keeper's ample garden'; a new garden open to the public was created in 1973. Prisoners were always locked up indoors, men downstairs, women upstairs. This or another bridewell may have been on the site of the former infants' school in Gaol Street (Market Street). There may also have been a bridewell in Gaol Lane (part of Barton Road) as some years ago a resident stated that the former Theological College, built 1881, was on the site of an 'old gaol'. Reference to a bridewell being 'against Barton Gate' until about 1852 may refer to that same building. There was a House of Correction, as these buildings were sometimes called, in Egremont Street c1855. Part of the building on the site of Old Hereward Hall was a bridewell for almost 10 years in the 17th century: this later became the Green Man public house, after Canon Hitch lived there.

The bridewell of 1651 presumably ceased to be used as a prison soon after 1820, as the Shire Hall, with a House of Correction, was built on the Lynn Road. Later, but now demolished, a separate House of Correction to the rear, with 35 cells, was built in 1843 and used for over 30 years. Ten years later there was much discussion as to whether the Ely Gaol should be closed so all prisoners could be accommodated at Wisbech and by 1865 the north wing of the Shire Hall and later the House of Correction were used by the Volunteers as an armoury. Today Shire Hall houses the Ely Citizens' Advice Bureau, the Magistrates' Court and, in part of the building used from 1847 to 1970 as the police station, a probation office.

Until 1841, when the Isle of Ely Constabulary, with a paid force headed by a chief constable (£200 per annun), had been formed, the enforcement of law and order had been in the hands of parish constables. The Isle force became part of the Mid Anglia Constabulary in 1965 and five years later moved into new premises, with an ambulance station next door, on the site of the former Holy Trinity vicarage. On the reorganisation of local government in 1974 the local force became part of the Cambridgeshire Constabulary.

RULES

TO BE OBSERVED BY THE

INMATES OF THE ALMS-HOUSES

OF

PARSONS' CHARITY.

1. The Inmates are not to take in Lodgers, nor to have any person residing with them without permission.

2. They are expected to attend Divine Service either at the Parish Church or at some other place of public worship, at least once on every Sunday, unless hindered by sickness or infirmity.

3. If it appears to the Governors desirable that any person should be removed from the Alms-houses they are at liberty to remove such person. If an inmate be removed for any other cause than misconduct, four weeks' notice of removal will be given.

4. The Alms-house Court is closed at Ten o'clock in the Evening between Lady-day and Michaelmas, and at Nine o'clock between Michaelmas and Lady-day. After the closing of the Gate no person is allowed to come in or go out until the following morning, except for some special reasons to be notified as early as possible to the Superintendent.

5. The Inmates are required to conduct themselves soberly and decently, and to abstain from all unseemly noise and strife, they must keep the rooms assigned to them in clean and wholesome condition, and use the sinks, drains, and offices to which they have access, in such manner as to prevent any nuisance therefrom or impediment therein.

6. The Governors or the Superintendent will visit the Alms-houses from time to time for the purpose of inspecting their condition.

7. No Inmate is allowed to be absent for more than seven days in succession without notifying to the Superintendent such absence and the cause thereof.

GOODWYN ARCHER,
Clerk to the Governors of Parsons' Charity.

Ely, November 29th, 1859.

Mrs CATHARINE NEEDHAM Widow of new Alresford in Hampshire originally of this Town who devised and bequeathed by her last will certain Estates in this Town & Neighbourhood of near Eighty Pounds per Annum for poor Boys born in the City of Ely of poor Parents for their Schooling Cloathing & putting them out Apprentices and towards their better Maintenance during the time of their going to School not exceeding five Years or in such other manner as RICHD STEVENS of ye Inner Temple Esqr Mr CORN GAY of ye City of Ely & Mr GEORGE HALL ye Trustees named in ye said will ye Survivors or Survivor of them should think fit and finally direct or their Successors should further order for ye better Execution of ye Trust in them reposed

LEFT: The initial from the Charles I charter which ordained 'that there should be one body corporate and politic . . . called by the name of the Governors of the Lands & Possessions of the Poor of Ely'. It was to consist of the Bishop, Dean, Archdeacon and nine citizens. (PC) BELOW: This board, which tells of the foundation of the school following the will of Catherine Needham in 1740, is still on the outside of the original Needham's School building on Back Hill. (BL) RIGHT: The Rules, 1859.

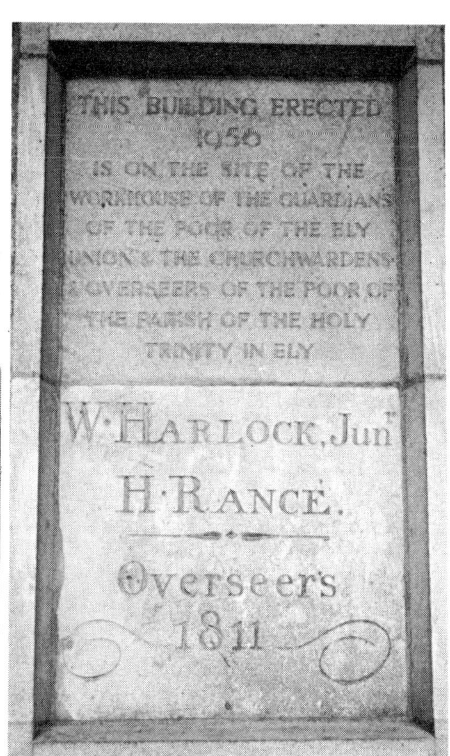

LEFT: The former Plough and Fleece on the site of St Mary's Workhouse, in use as the Kumin Cafe — the wooden teapot was once over the door and later stood on the pavement. BELOW: Holy Trinity Workhouse; the stone set into the wall between the windows RIGHT: was later put into the wall of a more recent building, demolished in 1989.

LEFT: The Union; east facade. (BL) RIGHT: Plan of the Union c1836; this is now incorporated into the larger Tower Hospital. (CC) BELOW: Nurse Clarke with VAD volunteers, c1940 — from the left, back row: Marjorie Woodroffe, Miss King, Mr Blake, Miss Maclean, Miss Garnett; centre back: —, Mrs Wright, Mrs Comber, —, Muriel Ambrose, —, Marjorie Aveling, Hilda Unwin, Miss Green; centre front: Mrs Nottage, —, Miss Collins, Nurse Clarke, Winifred Comins, Gladys Holmes, Mrs Cole; front: Miss Oakey, Miss Clow and Freda Street.

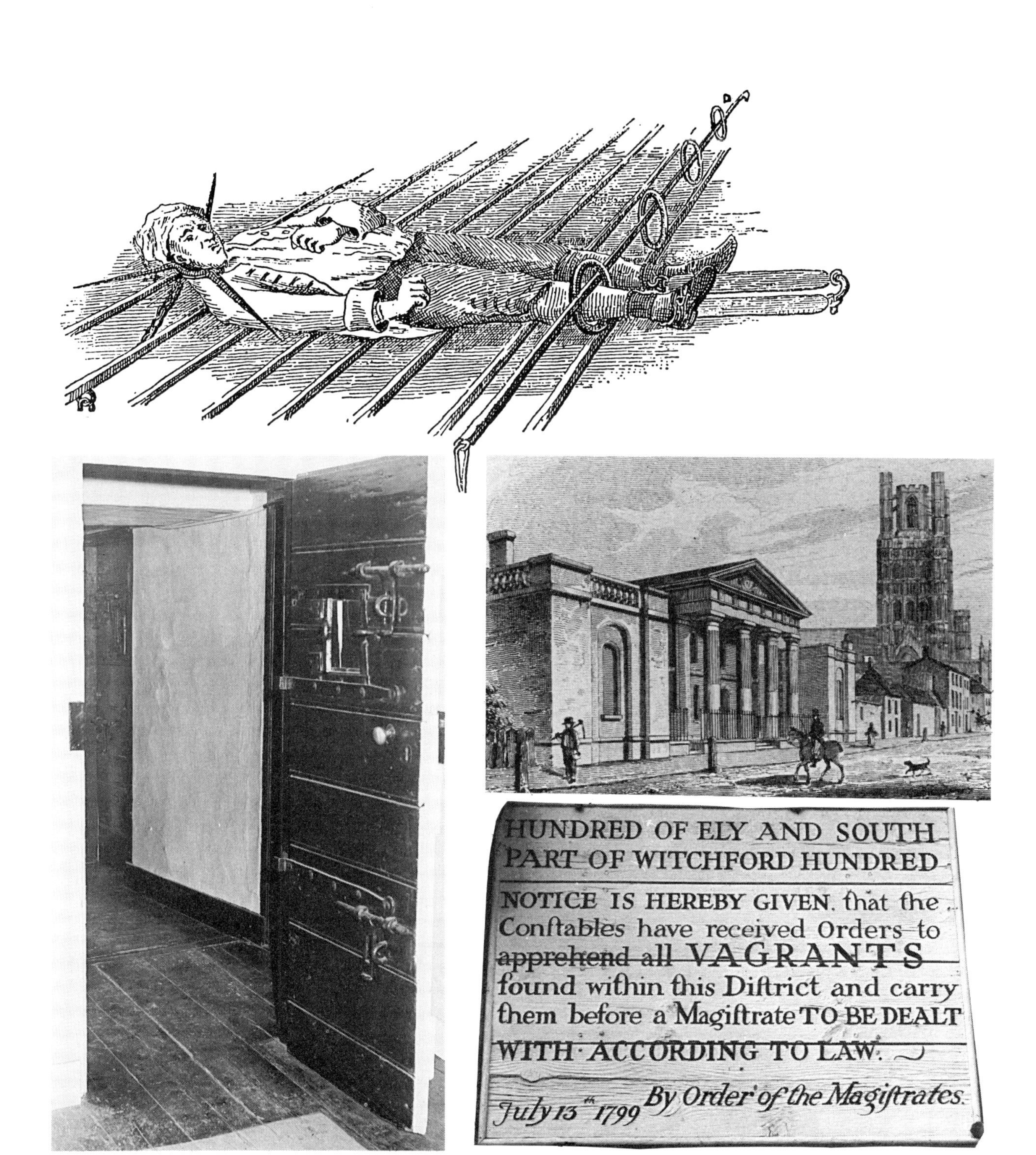

ABOVE: 'Torture inflicted in Ely Prison in 1768.' Prisoners in the Bishop's prison were chained to the floor, across which were several iron bars, with an iron collar with spikes about their necks, and a heavy iron bar across their legs. (CC) LEFT: A cell door still in position at the former Bishop's Gaol in Lynn Road on the corner of Market Street; part of the building is now used as the City of Ely Council Chamber, part as the office of the Registrar of Births, Deaths and Marriages. (CEN) RIGHT: This 19th century print of Lynn Road shows the Bishop's Gaol just beyond the third section of the Shire Hall. BELOW: This Board is a reminder that those who could not pay a settlement fee would not be allowed to stay in the parish.

Here lye Interred, in one grave
the Bodies of
WILLIAM BEAMISS,
GEORGE CROW,
JOHN DENNIS,
ISAAC HARLEY,
AND
THOMAS SOUTH,
Who were all executed at Ely on the 28
Day of June 1816, having been convicted
at the Special Assizes holden there, of
divers Robberies during the Riots at Ely
Littleport in the Month of May in that Year
May their awful Fate
be a warning to others

LEFT: The tablet set into the South wall of St Mary's Church tower, which commemorates those hanged in 1816 after the Ely and Littleport Riots. RIGHT: Unfortunately not a photograph of the 1939 fire, which was to the left of this picture, but only of the scene looking up Waterside: Colonel Archer, Chief Fire Officer, stands to the left of the engine. BELOW: The Fire Brigade outside the first Fire Station at Old Fire Engine House; the short, stocky fireman with the hose at his feet is Frederick Aveling of the Broad Street firm of painters & decorators.

Times of Trouble

Although the sacking of the monastery by the Danes and the defeat of Hereward by the Normans would no doubt have been considered disasters in Ely, both were local incidents, though part of larger, national events. Ely also played a part in the troubled times of the middle of the 12th century, when Matilda and Stephen vied for the throne of England. Bishop Nigel, who favoured Matilda's claim, was ordered to deliver Ely Castle, then recently built near present-day Castelhythe, to Stephen. He refused and was imprisoned but escaped and eventually returned to Ely. The castle was later held against the King for a time, before events moved elsewhere. Perhaps the most disastrous happening peculiar to Ely was the fall of the central Norman tower of the Cathedral.

Throughout the years there have been misfortunes, murder, drowning, fire, storm and the small disturbances, some documented, that occur at any time in most communities; monks in 1528 were said to have rushed furiously from the monastery 'not lyke any men of god relegyon' and struck down a child. A more important incident of 1217 was when Walter Buck with his Brabanters (Flemings) was said to have 'destroyed the Towne and Isle of Ely and almost burnt the Minstre therein . . .' but it was saved on 'payment of 209 marks' by the Prior.

Civil War reached the fens in the reign of Henry III when the group known as 'The Disinherited' came to the Isle of Ely in August 1266, and scoured the district for provisions. The Bishop's report to the King did not find favour; the King was thought to sympathise with the rebels. They remained until 1268 when Prince Edward and his soldiers entered the Isle 'after making bridges of wicker-work and planks, under the instruction of the inhabitants' and brought about the submission of The Disinherited. There is no record they entered Ely itself.

The Cathedral and monastery seem not to have attracted the riots and consequent destruction suffered in Bury St Edmunds and Norwich; when there was trouble it was usually initiated by outsiders. At Ely, during a century when the Lady Chapel and lantern tower were built, much other monastic building was in progress and the relatively small community was fully occupied. Again, Ely citizens were dependent on the 'abnormally powerful lordship' of the monastery, and 'feudalism so paternal could neither easily be outgrown nor overthrown'. 1381 saw Ely, according to the *Victoria County History*, as 'the centre of a far more violent uprising than in the rest of the shire' but it was limited to a few days. Ely man Richard de Leycester 'defying ecclesiastical authority mounted the cathedral pulpit', the Bishop's prison was attacked, and Sir Edmund Walsyngham, a justice, was executed and various rolls and documents destroyed. The rebels then met up with Robert Tavel of Lavenham near Ely High Bridge and moved to Ramsey.

The Undertakers, those who had undertaken to drain the fens, and the Adventurers who 'adventured' their money to finance this work provided a cause of strife peculiar to the fens during the 17th century, as the local people considered the drainage to be economically disastrous, preventing them from catching wild fowl and fish, cutting reeds, digging turf or pasturing their cattle; 'There's magic in a Common for those who depend on cattle for their living'. There were riots from all quarters in 1638, as the 'poor, desperate in heart, bethought themselves of fighting for their dinners'. Edward Powell *alias* Anderson stirred up Ely and Littleport men to meet, he said, to play a game of Camp Ball or Camping, a type of football, at Whelpmoor in the fen nearby intending 'to throw doune the ditch in Whelp-more wch the Undertakers made'. The first verse from *Powte's Complaint*, published 1662, illustrates feelings at the time:

> 'Come Brethren of the water, and let us all assemble,
> To treat upon this matter, which makes us quake and tremble;
> For we shall rue it if't be true that Fenns be undertaken,
> And where we feed in Fen and Reed thei'le feed both Beef and Bacon.'

Drainage schemes continued to attract local opposition throughout the Civil War, when Oliver Cromwell earned the title 'Lord of the Fens', as an opponent, not of drainage schemes themselves, but of the injustice done to the 'Commoners' who lost their rights.

Deserts rather than rights was perhaps the case when Amy Hutchinson was 'Burnt at the stake . . . in the city of Ely 1750' (after she had been strangled). She was said to be the first woman in England to be convicted of poisoning; the victim her husband.

'Food' riots occurred in Ely in 1757 and 1795 and a mutiny among local Militia men was suppressed in 1809 'by the arrival of four squadrons of the German Legion Cavalry' from Ipswich. Five ringleaders were flogged by the Germans and this so excited William Cobbett that he wrote an article denouncing the Government. He was prosecuted for libel, found guilty and sentenced to two years' imprisonment with a fine of £1,000.

More serious were the Ely and Littleport Riots of 1816. After a series of disturbances in East Anglia, labourers at Littleport, five miles from Ely, 'responding to low wages, unemployment, and high food prices' and other 'deeper grievances' attacked houses and people, then marched to Ely. Eventually Thomas Archer went on horseback to Bury St Edmunds to fetch a detachment of the First Royal Dragoon Guards to subdue and capture the rioters. The outcome was that over 50, including two women, stood trial and six were deported, 11 sent to prison, though ten of these were later deported, and five men were hanged at the gibbet in St John's Road.

Small fires from time to time have been reported; money was sent from nearby places, for example from Elton (Hunts) in 1702 'For a fire at the citty of Ely 5s 2d'. The report of an earlier fire at St John's Farm provides one of the few records of that part of Ely. The Cathedral had its share of small fires, one of which in 1779 occurred in a chamber near the lantern. By chance a carpenter discovered it and tore up the flaming boards, threw them down into the octagon and saved the tower, if not possibly the whole building. A number of haystack fires occurred, alarmingly close to buildings in the City centre. One such at 7.30 am on a day in 1834 was at Jonathan Page's premises at Cromwell House. The report stated that, had the fire been at night, 'the loss must have proved enormous, as large corn, hay and straw stacks were adjoining . . . besides the very large [tithe] barn full of corn, and being also surrounded with buildings . . .'. The engines, hand-drawn, were quickly on the spot and 'by the prompt assistance of the inhabitants' the fire was controlled. At the Chantry, home of John Muriel, surgeon, a fire behind his premises in St Mary's Street in the following year was quickly extinguished, due to prompt action by an employee of a nearby grocer and druggist who, 'with great presence of mind removed gunpowder from the warehouse . . . even before dressing himself'. April 1938 saw another fire, which could easily have proved disastrous, at Wright's butcher's shop next to Barclays Bank in High Street but typically, serious damage was confined to one building. Perhaps the City's most spectacular fire was that of Wednesday 27 September 1939 at disused brewery premises near the quay, when 137,000 bags stored for the Beet Sugar Factory went up in flames some 70 ft high. Mrs Daisy Rogers, who lived at Quayside in the former Haven said 'I thought it was the sunset when I saw the glow . . . but the noise of crackling and splintering glass followed and made me realise it was a fire. I rushed out to send for the fire brigade . . .'. Many people hurried down Waterside to watch and to share the excitement of such an unusual event. On that occasion Chief Fire Officer Colonel G.L. Archer was in charge.

It seems most likely and most fortunate that no serious fire took place in the City centre, certainly for several centuries; the age of the core of many central buildings confirms this and perhaps also the fact that a fire in which three haystacks were destroyed was thought by the local press to be a 'serious blaze'. The Fire Engine was kept at the present Old Fire Engine House Restaurant, with equipment in Church Lane and in the old belfry in High Street until 1912, when a suitable building and practice tower were erected on Lynn Road next to the Old Gaol. When the Urban District Council offices were re-built in 1931 the fire engine was 're-housed' below the Council chamber, until 1943. Headquarters then moved to Egremont Street, where a new fire station was erected in 1970; by 1982 a small museum had also been established. A Voluntary Brigade had been formed in 1877 and by 1904 an official one had been established.

In the matter of storms Ely seems again to have been fortunate. Earthquakes and tremors which caused little damage have also been recorded, though 1165 saw a 'great earthquake in Ely' said to overthrow 'them that stood upon their feete, and made the bels to ring'. Another earthquake of 1692 was said to have been the cause of damage to the north-west corner of the north transept of the Cathedral. Another, 'The greatest storm of any that had happened for some time past . . . demolished the vane of the cathedral . . . with part of the stonework of the turret' (1776) and in 1860 'a considerable portion of the beautiful large chestnut trees' planted c1780 by Canon Bentham near the Porta was 'carried off'. Another great storm on the night of 15/16 October 1987 almost by-passed Ely, though some trees fell, and lead on the Cathedral roof was lifted.

The weather was also partly responsible for the floods that occurred, often in spring, when the tow-path from Ely High Bridge to the Cutter was submerged, houses on Babylon were seriously flooded and some Ely people could not but be aware of the worst of the floods in the surrounding fen. 1947 saw Ely in the forefront of the battle to 'save the banks' which overflowed and were breached in several places, the nearest at Little Thetford. A total of nearly 25,000 acres was flooded. The Army was called in to assist and its headquarters for 'Operation Noah's Ark' were in the Preparatory Department of the Girls' High School; the pupils who normally used this part of the school had two weeks' holiday.

At the end of the 18th century Ely had its Loyal Association of Volunteers 'to resist revolution and possible invasion'. Around then four companies of the Nottinghamshire Militia marched to Ely from Cambridge and expected to stay for the winter. This was at a time when a man called for military service was allowed, if he paid the current rate of £3 3s 0d, to provide a substitute; many local men did so. *The Cambridge Chronicle* (1860) stated that, although Ely was once proverbial for being a century behind other places, 'such an assertion now would be a positive insult; for great improvements, and keeping pace with the spirit of the age Ely is by no means inferior to other places'. So began an account of the formation of a Volunteer Rifle Corps in Ely, agreed at a meeting chaired by the Dean. After an application made by the CO of the Cambridgeshire Militia 'Her Majesty graciously bestowed on the city of Ely' a Russian cannon used against British forces at Sebastopol in the Crimean War. It was brought to Ely by rail, 26 June 1860 accompanied, not as expected by the band of the Coldstream Guards, but by that of the Grenadiers, and dragged by a team of six horses to the Palace Green. Here the somewhat rusty cannon was installed with difficulty due to the muddy ground and stands today well polished by generations of children's backsides. Fantastic stories that the gun was used by Oliver Cromwell on Stuntney Hill to attack Ely, that he used it to keep the Dean and Chapter in order, that it demolished the north-west transept and so on, abound. That June day was also marked by a Flower Show in the grounds of the Bishop's Palace.

The Militia transformed social life from 1860 until this volunteer force changed to a Territorial one and left Ely in 1908. From its inception, Ely had been the headquarters of the Cambridgeshire Militia, which later became part of the Suffolk Regiment. 'Ely's society was miniscule' so the townspeople eagerly welcomed Cambridgeshire Militia officers. Lord Colin Campbell, perhaps a guest from another regiment, provided a particularly distinguished dancing partner for young ladies in the 1870s, one of whom, Jeanette Marshall, frequently visited her aunt and uncle at Etheldreda House, then Hill House, on Back Hill. The Officers' Mess at the Lamb Hotel was the scene of many gay and noisy evenings; on Guest Nights the regimental band played at the nearby street corner and attracted a large crowd, which included 'young roughs' who created 'a perfect pandemonium'. The late Lt Col Archer said in his notes that 'there was . . . no difficulty obtaining private billets as the popularity of the local Red Coat was considerable' but unfortunately 'human souvenirs' were apt to appear some nine months later. Particularly when training coincided with the May Fair, 'riotous scenes took place as belts were flourished and fights broke out in the streets'. Although the men were billetted out for many years more, permanent headquarters were built in 1869 off Silver Street to house the sergeants. Known as the Range, it and the former hospital building, remain today.

Billetting also took place during World War II – even before it began, from 1 September 1939 – when the first evacuees arrived. The High School for Girls in Ely shared its premises, and part of Archer House and a large room at the back of the Club Hotel with the Central Foundation School from Bishopsgate, London. A farewell party in July 1943 officially celebrated the return of the school to its London home. During the war the Jews' Free School was also accommodated in the City at Old Hereward Hall in The Gallery. Lasting friendships were made and some Ely foster-parents are still in touch with their former evacuees.

The greatest hardship caused in Ely by the wars of the last 200 years has been loss of life; many men of the Cambridgeshires were in Singapore when it fell to the Japanese in 1942, many died and many were imprisoned until 1945, including one of Ely's most distinguished citizens of this century, Lt Col John Beckett. He played a courageous role as, through a small radio receiver constructed in his water bottle, and an illicit newspaper, he was able to spread news of the war, essential for prisoners' morale, throughout the camp. After his return to Ely and his peacetime solicitor's practice, he became a County, District and Parish Councillor, High Sheriff for Cambridgeshire 1966/7, Mayor of Ely 1977/8 and first honorary alderman of the District Council. John Goodwyn Allden Beckett OBE TD DL MA (Cantab) died aged 73, 12 November 1987.

The two wars of this century led to changes which were countrywide – the need to nurse convalescent service men, the formation of the Local Defence Volunteers later to become the Home Guard, the appointment of Air Raid Wardens and the organisation of a number of fund-raising efforts – but in Ely little or no war damage. During World War I zeppelins passed over Ely, one in February 1916 so low that members of the crew could be plainly seen. This was 'one of ours' and so not referred to as a 'Baby-killer', as were those which took part in the 'great air raid' on East Anglia during the same month. In World War II, isolated bombs fell on most roads leading to Ely but, with two or three exceptions, were too far from the centre to cause damage to people or property. On 19 June 1940 eight high explosive bombs fell in the

West Fen area of Ely, damaged a hut, killed 30 cattle and one civilian. In November nine bombs fell on the Beet Sugar Factory; 16 workers were injured and sufficient damage done for the factory to be closed for a month. A German 'plane came down near Stuntney in the same year and, it is said, a man was killed when a bomb fell near the gates of the RAF Hospital. From an RAF aerodrome two miles from the City centre off the A10, which opened in June 1943, Wellington, Stirling and Lancaster bombers operated. The 'softening of the Ruhr' in preparation for the 1944 Normandy invasion and during the next year 'Food Drops' to Holland, where large areas had been flooded by the Germans, were carried out. The aerodrome was left vacant in August 1945 and early the next year it closed.

A prisoner-of-war camp had been established in the fields of Barton Farm; here Italians and later Germans were securely held, though the former were allowed into the City centre and to the cinema. The camp later housed refugees, before it was closed and the pre-war picnic area was converted into a golf course.

Typical fund-raising efforts were the 1941 War Weapons Week which, with the slogan 'The Fen Tigers Go To It', raised £300,117, and a Warship Week held in March 1942, which raised £259,000. This led to the adoption of HMS *Walpole* by the City; in 1989 the ship's battle ensign was laid up in Ely Cathedral where it hangs in the north transept. The ship's bell is in Ely Museum and on 20 October 1989 one of the ship's plaques, found in an American antique shop, was presented to the museum.

Undoubtedly the greatest benefit brought by war was the hurried erection, on land once part of New Barns Farm, of the RAF Hospital. It was awarded the Freedom of the City in 1977 and, on the occasion when that freedom was first exercised, the Red Arrows flew over Ely in salute.

The first of the Lynn Road Fire Stations next to the Bishops prison (Old Gaol).

LEFT: The next move was a few yards along Lynn Road to accommodation below the new UDC offices. Here the High Sheriff reads the proclamation of the Accession of George VI in 1936. (CC) RIGHT: Flood water near the Cutter Inn and, on the right, two of the last cottages on Babylon, c1927. BELOW: The tow path which leads toward Ely. (The water has risen to flood the wash land between the embankments, a common occurrence in the spring during the first half of this century, until flood protection was improved from 1954 onwards.)

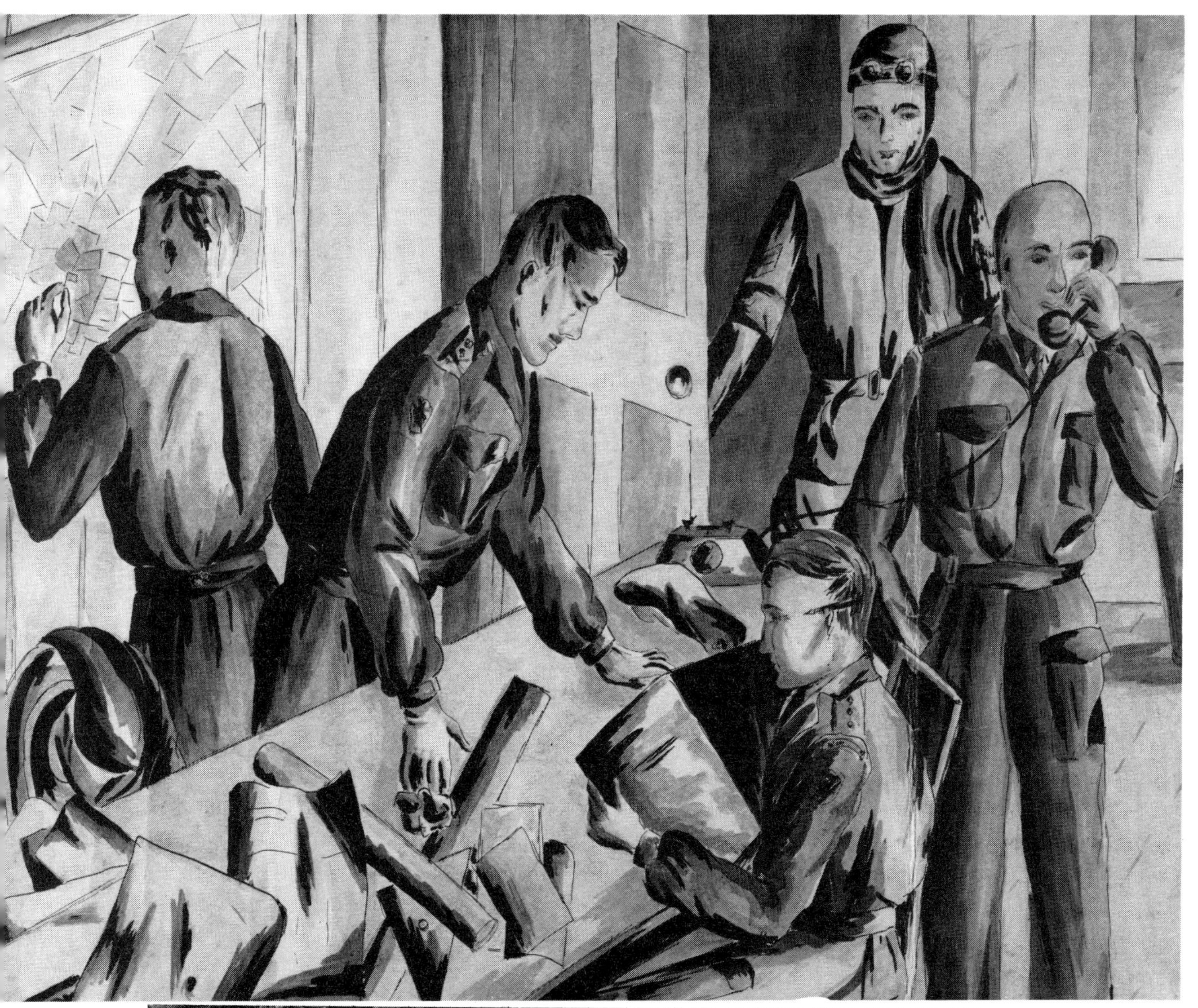

ABOVE: Operation Noah's Ark, March 1947. BELOW: The cannon in Palace Green; it points away from the cathedral.

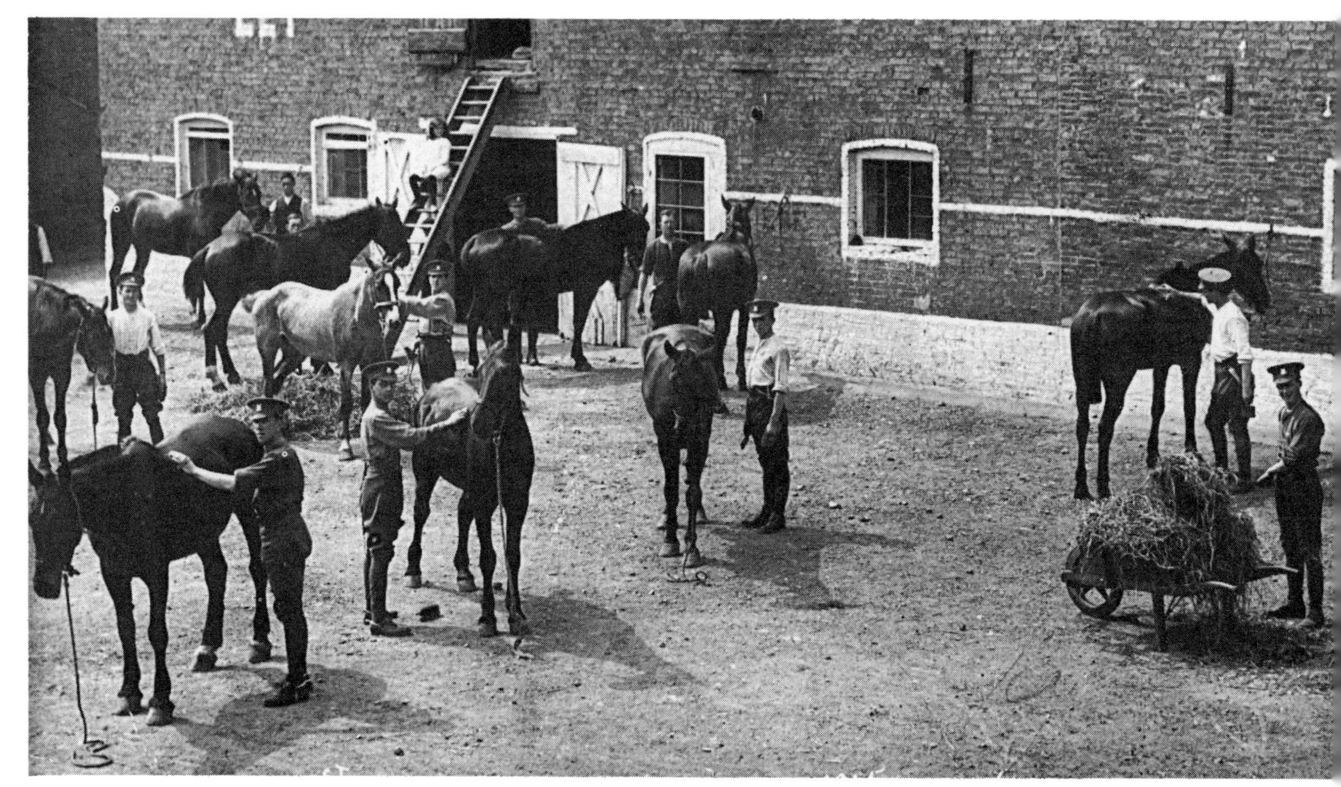

ABOVE: 'The 2/1st Suffolk Yeomanry departure from Ely June 11, 1915' — soldiers preparing to leave from the old granary, which stood near the river on the southern side of Annesdale, before town houses were built there. BELOW: Colonel Beckett heads a column of survivors of the 2nd Battalion of the Cambridgeshire Regiment, who had recently returned from Japanese PoW camp in 1945. (MR)

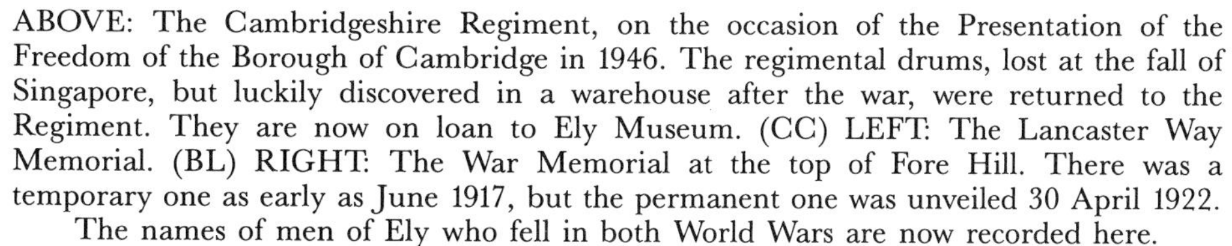

ABOVE: The Cambridgeshire Regiment, on the occasion of the Presentation of the Freedom of the Borough of Cambridge in 1946. The regimental drums, lost at the fall of Singapore, but luckily discovered in a warehouse after the war, were returned to the Regiment. They are now on loan to Ely Museum. (CC) LEFT: The Lancaster Way Memorial. (BL) RIGHT: The War Memorial at the top of Fore Hill. There was a temporary one as early as June 1917, but the permanent one was unveiled 30 April 1922. The names of men of Ely who fell in both World Wars are now recorded here.

ABOVE: Celebrations at Ely on 15 July 1814. The company assembled in High Street and on the Market Place and at 11.00 am a stage decorated with laurels, roses etc carried by 12 men, emerged from the Red Lion. On the stage was Mrs Playford, impersonating Britannia with a 'lion' at her feet; this headed the procession to the Nutholt (near the present Nutholt Lane) where a transparency had been placed at the entrance. Later the transparency was carried in procession to the Cathedral where it was set up and lighted. The jollifications went on until midnight and continued the next day. BELOW: The transparency was 'a device on some translucent substance, made visible by means of a light behind.'

Celebration

The translation of the body of St Etheldreda by her sister Sexburgha on 17 October 695, must have been one of the earliest celebrations of importance. After this event, pittances then in the form of money, were given by benefactors to provide extra food on particular occasions; they were received by the monks on this day each year, on the anniversary of the burial of St Withburga and on other feast days. The accounts of the Pitanciarius give little information but mention money spent on sturgeon, full-grown pike, whelks, lampreys, merling and salmon. During the 14th century a particular type of 'Tartys' made with pork, eggs, figs and spices in a pastry case was regarded as a delicacy.

The menu for the meal provided after the installation of John Morton as Bishop of Ely in 1479 suggests that this was indeed a celebration of 'great State and Magnificence'. The first course included soup, frumenty (hulled wheat boiled in milk and seasoned), venison, 'syngnet rosted, Fesant roosted': the second, peacock, carp, rabbit, bream and the third 'creme of Almondes' soup, perch, curlew, plover and larks roasted; fresh sturgeon, quinces in paste and various tarts, custards and cakes were also served. Present at the feast were the Abbots of Thorney, Bury and Ramsey, the Priors of Ely, Barnwell and Anglesey, the Master of the Rolls, Sir Thomas Howard 2nd Duke of Norfolk and other titled people and 'gentry'.

Undoubtedly one of the most alarming and dangerous celebrations must have been the Thanksgiving of 1789 to mark the recovery from illness of George III. 'At Ely, an anthem, composed for the occasion by Mr. Skeats the organist was performed . . . and in the evening the city in general was illuminated. The dome or lantern of the cathedral made a most brilliant appearance; a frame of wood was ingeniously contrived for the occasion, by Mr. Winter, carpenter, on which were fixed six hundred candles; on its going up, the bells rang, the organ played, and *God save the King* was sung by the choir, the same on its being taken down . . .'

The cessation of war, coronations and jubilees have been and are the cause for celebration in Ely as elsewhere. The peace at the end of the Napoleonic Wars was as in many places celebrated prematurely on 14 July 1814. The first celebration, a grand official occasion, is recorded in a large aquaint which shows the scene on the Nutholt; the names of citizens who contributed financially to the day's jollifications were also listed. On the day 'A most excellent Dinner of very rich Plum Puddings and Beef of the first Quality was' eaten by about 3,000 people. 'After Dinner an abundance of good strong Ale, and Pipes and Tobacco, were distributed and many loyal and appropriate Toasts given'. *Rule Britannia* was sung, there were 'Rural Sports' – donkey races and amusements – until 8.00 pm, bands played, dancing took place and a firework display continued until after midnight. The second celebration took place at the large premises, suitably decorated with 'transparencies, varigated lamps, laurels etc.', of the 'King of Babylon', boatwright John Pond. He too provided plum puddings, with legs of mutton, for about 150 people and, after bonfires, fireworks and other celebrations had continued all night, a public breakfast. This jollification was followed by two nights of dancing.

The remembrance of St Etheldreda has continued and, after the 1873 Festival, an illustrated historical summary by Dean Merivale was published. This festival began on 17 October with Litany at 9.00 am and ended on 21 October in the evening. Services were interspersed with a 'Luncheon at the Bishop's Palace for the Clergy of the Isle of Ely', an evening entertainment – at the Lamb for College workers, tenants and tradesmen, at the Bell Hotel for School Managers and Teachers, at their school for the choristers, at the Corn Exchange for bedesmen, college servants, parents of National School children and others – an organ recital by Dr Chipp, cathedral organist and a lecture in the Cathedral by Sir George Gilbert Scott (delivered by his son). A 'sumptuous luncheon' was held 'for invited guests' in the Corn Exchange, 'gay with flags and mottoes', among whom were the Archbishop of Canterbury, and the Vice-Chancellor of the University of Cambridge.

On the final day choirs from the diocese joined the Cathedral choir, 676 'certified singers' processed down the nave, accompanied by the band of the Cambridgeshire Militia, and 'the brightness of the brass instruments, combined with the vigorous beat of the drum' kept the voices together. Festivities closed with 'Tea for the Choirs in the Corn Exchange'.

The 12th centenary of the foundation of the monastery had been well celebrated but the 13th centenary led to one of the most exciting years in Ely's history. Cathedral and City united to celebrate and to give thanks for their past. Festivities began with a bang as 4 March 1973 was a day of rain, hail, snow, thunder and lightning. The Dean, Very Rev Michael Carey, accompanied by the Bishop, opened the celebrations outside the Cathedral in the presence of over 4,000 people and the Queen's Division Training Regiment Band, who played a fanfare. At the Waterside 50 ladies took part in a pancake race and a display of Morris Dancing was staged.

The Cathedral, the streets and the river provided the setting for many services and events throughout the year, which ranged from concerts, exhibitions, displays, tournaments, sports events, an Inland Waterways National Boat Rally, flower festivals, a schools' Art and Craft Exhibition, a Street Festival and BBC Gardeners Question Time to the TV contest *It's a Knockout*. The Ely team had 'taken on' in turn Hertford and then teams from Switzerland, Germany, the Netherlands, Italy, Belgium and France. When almost unbelievably Ely, unbeaten in the series, *won*, there could have been few in the City who did not share the excitement; although only a television game, that success became symbolic of the year. The Street Festival provided another unforgettable experience: traffic was banned from the central streets and, on a clear, bright and warm 15 May, about 6,000 children came by coach and by special train to take part, another 2,000 or so to watch.

Again the date of St Etheldreda's death and translation of 23 June 679 was particularly commemorated by the Bishop of Ely and the Bishop of Huntingdon with their 300 mile tour around the Diocese, culminating in the Cathedral where the Archbishop of Canterbury, Michael Ramsay gave the sermon.

Of the many musical events one was not officially part of the Festival; on 1 September Leonard Bernstein conducted Mahler's Second Symphony in the Cathedral when it was filmed for American television.

Officially the celebrations ended on 20 October with a Festival of Praise, when St Etheldreda who 'began that tradition of Christian worship and witness in which we stand and about which we rejoice' was remembered, but there was however a second finale when, on 23 November, Her Majesty Queen Elizabeth II visited Ely – a fitting climax to an 'exciting, wonderful and memorable' period in the history of the City.

The Appeal for £4m to restore the Cathedral led to several festive fund-raising occasions, the 1987 Flower Festival probably the most important. Members of Flower Clubs throughout

East Anglia, led by Lorna Henwood, displayed flowers in a great variety of ways to enhance the stonework, and to complement the stained glass. The three day festival was opened on the evening of 9 July by the Princess of Wales.

The following year His Royal Highness Prince Philip, Duke of Edinburgh, patron of the appeal, attended a service to mark its success and in November 1989 he was present at the Restoration Thanksgiving Service.

Queen Elizabeth's second official visit, accompanied by the Duke of Edinburgh, was for the distribution of the Royal Maundy in the Cathedral, Thursday 16 April 1987. Then 61 men and 61 women, the same number as the sovereign's lifespan, received a white purse containing six specially minted sets of silver 4p, 3p, 2p and 1p coins plus one penny and a red purse containing a £5 note and a 50p piece, which replaced the one-time gift of clothing. Nosegays were carried by the chief participants, including four Ely 'Children of the Royal Almonry'; they received a set of money as their 'fee'. Recipients of the Royal Maundy, usually elderly and chosen for their service to Church or community, were men and women of the diocese; among Ely citizens were Miss Lucy Brunning, Mr Leonard Jackman, Mr Ted Haylock (churchwarden of St Mary's for nearly 20 years), Mr George Street, Mr Christopher King and Mr Arthur Balaam; others successfully avoided publicity. After the service Queen Elizabeth, and the Duke of Edinburgh, walked down The Gallery where she talked to many people.

For many years the various Friendly Societies organised a fund-raising parade in aid of Addenbrooke's Hospital, Cambridge and Hunstanton Convalescent Home, but this ended after the introduction of the National Health Service in 1948. In 1962 Hospital Sunday was re-instituted and, organised by the Friends of Tower Hospital, it has become an annual fund-raising event.

The Fountain placed on the Market Place to commemorate Queen Victoria's 1897 Jubilee seen here c1910 on Market Day. It was moved in 1939 to nearby Archery Crescent.

ABOVE: Conservative Dinner at the Bell Hotel March, 1957; standing: Bill Evans, George Comins, Sir Harry Legge-Bourke MP, Philip Cutlack, Daisy Rogers, Reg Houghton etc. Sir Harry was the Member for the Isle of Ely for 28 years during the period 1918-1983 when the Isle of Ely had separate Parliamentary representation. (BL) BELOW: The excitement in Paris after Ely won the European Knockout 1973. (ES)

ABOVE: The Street Festival 1973. (BL) LEFT: The logo for 1973. BELOW: Queen Elizabeth II talks to local people near the Maltings, 23 November 1973. Near the centre, Cllr Ron Meadows and Mrs Cooper enjoy their view of the proceedings. (CEN)

ABOVE: The Royal Maundy: David Lawrence, Emily Lawrence, Samantha King and Adam O'Loughlin stand to either side of the Queen and the Duke of Edinburgh. Behind are members of the Dean and Chapter and the Bishop of Ely, the Right Reverend Peter Walker, 1987. (DC) BELOW: Her Majesty on the way to lunch escorted by the Lord Lieutenant of the County, 1987.

ABOVE: The Princess of Wales in her visit, 9 July 1987, to open the Ely Cathedral Festival of Flowers, after which she attended evensong in the Lady Chapel. (ES) BELOW: Coronation Day 1937; a photo taken in the 'Jam' Factory of a group ready to celebrate.

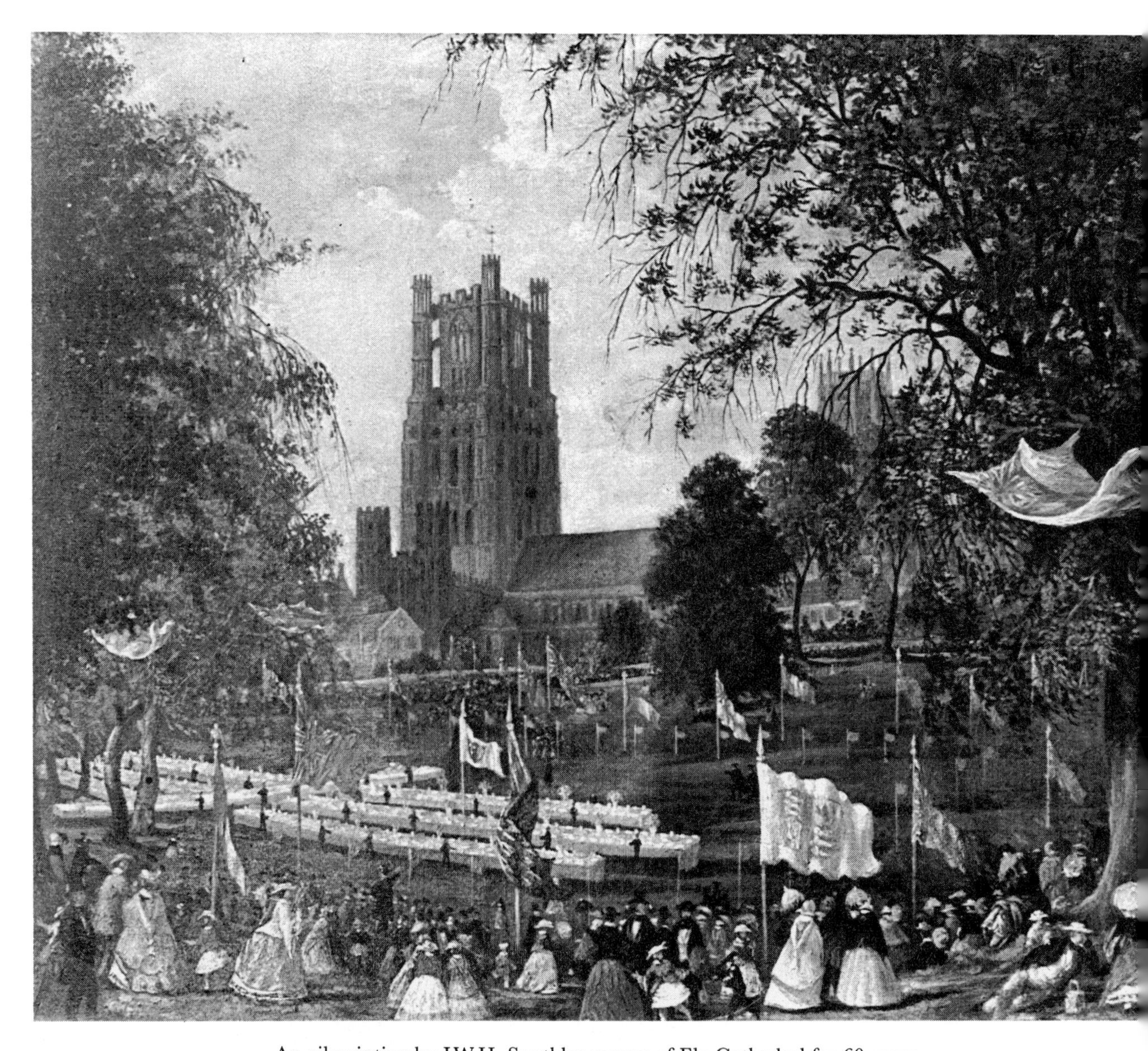

An oil painting by J.W.H. Southby, verger of Ely Cathedral for 60 years, of the luncheon in the Dean's Meadow in 1863, to mark the marriage of Princess Alexandra of Denmark to Albert Edward, Prince of Wales. (BL and DC).

Part of Ely's celebrations for the Coronation of Elizabeth II, 1953. Leading a group of Littleport 'rioters' with tricorn hat is Reg Holmes, the local historian.

ABOVE: Another Tom Bolton photo, taken in High Street on Peace Day, 1918. BELOW: Hospital Sunday 1920: this Tom Bolton photo was taken in the yard off Broad Street that led to Blakeman's factory; to the left is the side of Jones' sweet shop and behind the float the shop at that time, M.A. Briggs, later (c1933) J.M. Evans, respectively ladies' and gentlemen's clothiers.

Fun and Games

Leisure was rare and shortlived when fen folk struggled to make a living, rose early and went to bed early. No doubt some derived pleasure from hunting, fishing and wildfowling but these were necessary pursuits. Too often children had to work hard but doubtless found amusement in games and diversions. Later the play of children in more affluent circumstances is reflected by Henry Gunning's reminiscences of the small 17th century school where he was 'taught by a clergyman living in The College'. 'Our play-ground was very extensive; we had the range of the whole college. In bad weather we sheltered ourselves in the Cathedral, and, incredible as it may seem, we spun our tops & trundled our hoops without interruption. These practises have long since been abolished . . .'. One practice – that of hoop trundling – was revived in 1979 and has become a yearly event among King's School pupils.

Bandy was 'a forerunner of golf dating from the 14th century' but in Cambridgeshire it originated some four centuries later as a form of ice-hockey. It took place within a radius of about 17 miles from Bury Fen so may have been played by Ely folk. Camp Ball, a form of football, was certainly played in the Ely area.

Skating in the fens goes back many centuries; FitzStephen in 1180 said 'when the great fenne . . . is frozen, many young people play upon the yce . . . some tye bones to their feet and under their heels and . . . doe slide as swiftly as a bird flyeth in the air or an arrow out of a cross-bow'. Accounts of 19th century skating matches tell of popular venues close to Ely; Middle Fen Drain and, in unusually cold winters such as that of 1857 a 'fine piece of ice close to Ely Bridge, on the Washes'. This brought 'a great many gentlemen & others from Cambridge & the locality' and several races took place. Doubtless some had skated the 16 miles on the river from Cambridge as they did during 1929 and 1963. Perhaps not all had arrived on the characteristic fen 'runners', the blades made of iron, or performed in the characteristic fen manner, leaning well forward with hands and arms either behind the back or flailing vigorously. Unfortunately, towards the end of the 19th century, there was nowhere suitable at Ely where the popular races, once won by Fenland champions 'Turkey' and James Smart, C.W. Horn and Albert Tebbit, could take place.

Coursing is still a popular local sport though perhaps less so than when the Isle of Ely Coursing Club was formed, around the beginning of the 20th century, by a group of prominent local farmers and businessmen. Many Boxing Day meetings were held at Quanea Fen between Ely and Stuntney, in the days when Artful Dodger, owned by the uncle of club secretary Harold Trett, was the most notable dog to pursue, but not necessarily to kill, the hare.

The Cambridge boat race crew for many years used the three mile stretch of river near Queen Adelaide on which to practise, and there during World War II a Boat Race took place. This was won by Oxford, as was the first of 1829 which Charles Merivale, later Dean of Ely, helped to organise and in which he rowed. Today many King's School eights and pairs use the river near Ely, where both school and University have boat-houses on the Babylon side.

Pleasure trips on the river are associated with *The Viscountess Bury*, built 1888, and still used as a pleasure craft and *The Pattie*, no longer on the river. Many boats, mostly power-craft, are now moored, both along the river bank and in the Babylon marinas, but sailing craft are to be found at Roswell Pits. Here, in an area where the Kimmeridge clay has been dug out, the Ely Sailing Club has its headquarters. Founded in 1946, its craft first sailed on the river to the south of Ely High Bridge.

The 'Scandal and Disgrace' of the river near The Quay and towards the railway bridge south of Ely was not remedied until 1934. Neither clean nor safe, these were the only available places for bathing. Then a pool, where mixed bathing was allowed, was opened on the site of former filter beds near Station Road; in the same year Ely Swimming Club, successor to Ely River Club, was established. Four years later the mile-long (three quarters for ladies) swim in the river was organised by the Club. This was not an annual event, for the seventh and final Swim Through Ely took place on 17 July 1973; such a race could not continue in the polluted waters of the Ouse. Today Aquafast has been held annually since 1977 near Willow Walk and on the river.

With more leisure, fishing trips and matches became popular; the Coopers' Arms, the Marquis of Granby, the Cutter and the Highflyer had keen clubs for many years. Fishermen, mainly from Sheffield, were frequent and there were some 2,000 visitors during 1914. The Kimberley in Broad Street continued to provide accommodation until demolished to make way for the NFU Agriculture House, opened September 1980. Dace, roach, pike, perch, tench, bream, zander and eels have been caught during this century; eel pie and smoked eel are served at the Old Fire Engine House Restaurant today.

The 19th century saw a great increase in sporting and other activities. Amateur Dramatics, opera, concerts, bands, dances, societies, lectures, libraries, clubs, dances, fêtes and outings all abounded, but musical events particularly proliferated, both in City and Cathedral. During 1989 there were over 30 musical events in the Cathedral from April to October; with the Lady Chapel open again there are likely to be many more and during June 1990 a season of subscription concerts is being held to celebrate that.

Soon after the Militia left Ely a town band was formed; following the First World War, a Great Eastern Railway Band, and later a British Legion Band. Yet by the 1960s the City had none at all. Then the City of Ely Military Band was formed. On three occasions it has participated in the Lord Mayor's Show in London.

Ely Operatic Society attracted many local singers from its inception in 1910 until its closure in 1959. Among early singers were Pattie Legge and W. Cobb while later performers included Winifrid and Archie Haylock, Andrew Henderson, Alan Franklin (Norwich Cathedral chorister and, for over 30 years, Ely Cathedral verger), Charles Bush, Dorothy Fyson, Tom Coates and Tom Kempton; the men, except Tom Kempton, who incidentally was Chief Fire Officer for nearly 30 years, were Cathedral lay clerks. Other groups included the War Aid Singers, the City of Ely Orchestra and, before World War I, the Dandies. The St Mary's Chamber Choir and 'Shades of Blue' are two groups active today; the first conducted by a former lay clerk and the latter composed of present lay clerks.

The Working Men's Club and Institute held an embryo Sports Day in 1880 though small events, 'Rural Sports', had been held before that. The first 'Ely Sports' meeting was held at Paradise on August Bank Holiday 1893; this event continued, apart from two short breaks during the World Wars, until 1964. At one time the Sports were described as the 'premier athletic meeting of the Eastern Counties'; the cycling programme attracted world-class competitors, from the Horn brothers in the 1920s and '30s to Reg Harris in 1955. On Paradise, for many years the centre of sporting activity in Ely, football, cricket, tennis and hockey have been played and, in April 1986, the Paradise Leisure Centre opened, with a swimming pool and facilities for many indoor sports and activities, including judo, squash, roller skating, yoga and badminton.

Bowling was already popular in the City during the last century, when the White Hart boasted a green behind its Market Place premises. Now there is one at both the Beet Sugar Factory Club on Lynn Road and at the club in Nutholt Lane. This opened in 1925 and here the Ely Indoor Bowls Club had four rinks 20 years ago and now, with over 800 members, has six.

In Ely sport has also included archery, boxing – Eric Boon fought there – and golf, which has been played on Barton Fields since the early 1960s, though earlier in the 1920s on Prickwillow Road. The present course, officially opened in November 1962, is on the site of fields, once part of Barton Farm, used by many families for picnics, play and Sunday afternoon walks, before it became a prisoner-of-war camp during the 1940s. There also once were examples of the relatively few wild flowers within the City area; cowslips flourished but are now rarely found near Ely. Ely Park has provided an area for walking and playing games for many years, yet no lease between the Dean and Chapter and Ely UDC existed until 1964. Nearby Cherry Hill, perhaps originally the motte of a Norman castle, was a place for local youth to explore until it was fenced during the early 1980s. Now it acts as a nature reserve where, with permission, wild flowers, trees and birds can be studied.

Alehouses and inns were visited by monks as well as townspeople in the early 16th century. In the 17th, licensees had to conform to stringent regulations: the landlord was not permitted to 'have any playing at the cards, dice tables, Quoyts, loggetts, boules, or any other unlawful game or games in his house, yard, garden or backside' and no drinking was allowed during 'the tyme of divine prayers on the Sabboth daye'. By early 19th century, conditions of licensing had changed little but the list of banned games included draughts, bagatelle and 'Bull, Bear or Badger-baiting, Cock-fighting or other such sports . . .'. A 1714 inventory records the Lamb Hotel had a 'Cock Chamber', where fighting was illegally practised at the end of that century. A fat hog was the prize. Around the beginning of the 19th century Ely had at least 70 public houses but not all had licences to sell wines and spirits.

A Mechanics' Institute opened in 1842 and an Ely Museum in 1849, both at the premises of Marshall Fisher, librarian of the former, curator of the latter and, with George Bard, an Ely draper, responsible for its formation. The Institute, with 120 members, arranged lectures and had a library of nearly 2,000 volumes. The museum offered a first-class subscription at £1, others at 10s and 5s, while members non-resident in Ely paid 1s entrance fee, others 6d. On Fisher's death in 1899 the local council was not in a position to purchase the contents; a situation comparable to that when Vernon Cross's collection was auctioned in 1964. This had been started by his father, and included local fossils, old rifles, swords, pots, coins, traditional smocks, landworkers' cotton bonnets and innumerable other objects; it was housed in Ye Olde Tea Rooms on Fore Hill, a popular restaurant and baker's shop. Some of these exhibits can still be seen in the present Ely Museum, established by the Vernon Cross Trust at Sacrist's Gate in the High Street. This was opened by Ely's first 20th century Mayor, Cllr Fred Tucker, in 1975 and re-opened nearby, after almost two years' closure due to modernisation, on 8 September 1989, by Mayor Cllr Percy Powles.

Vernon Cross was a man of many parts – one time President of the National Association of Master Bakers, ventriloquist, keep-fit enthusiast, amateur actor, Urban District Councillor for almost 20 years and author; his book *Cross Words* (1972) reflects his distinctive character. The Ely Amateur Dramatic Society occupied much of his time during the 1920s, when he acted and produced. This society, still producing plays today, probably opened in 1888 – the year it produced *The Spitalfield Weaver*. Among others who shared Vernon Cross's enthusiasm and appeared on the stage in the Corn Exchange and in the Public Room were Gladys Woolnough, Mab Briggs, Reg Houghton and his wife, Frank Wilkinson, George Comins and Dr Maurice-Smith. Today performances take place in Needham's Hall; many post-war actors – Geoffrey and Stephen Legge, Ann Dix, Raymond Bailey, Tony Ransome – will be remembered. There have been and are other drama groups, such as those of the Women's Institutes and the Campaign Amateur Theatre. During the mid-19th century there was a Theatre Royal, run by the Militia, in 'Mr Legge's Auction-room, Newnham'. When the officers performed for the first time the historical drama *Charles XII* and *Box and Cox* they had 'a fashionable and full house'. Towards the end of the century, Douglas's theatre was at the Corn Exchange for nine days; 'always well patronised . . . and effectively staged'.

Itinerant entertainers were common; 1759, for example, saw Messrs Durravan's Company of Comedians in Ely, to entertain 'the Gentry and others' with select plays and, later in the same year, M. Powell 'the celebrated fire-eater' performed in a 'commodius room at the Bell Inn'. The Martin Harvey Company performed *Tobias and the Angel* and other plays when on visits to the High School for Girls during the 1930s.

Today drama is encouraged by the Ely Arts Association, which brought Eastern Angles, a professional company to the Maltings, to stage a play based on Graham Swift's 1983 novel *Waterland*; both book and play vividly recreated the 18th century fenland atmosphere.

Along with the rest of the country a revolution in leisure took place between the two World Wars, with the growth of the cinema. In Ely, under enterprising photographer Tom Bolton, the Ely Bioscope Co showed films in Victoria Hall during 1909, and again for a year from March 1911. The Ely Electric Cinema opened in 1912 in premises in Market Street, where later the Eastern Counties Omnibus Co had its offices. Here silent films were shown until the building of the Rex Cinema in 1929. This was soon re-modelled with a balcony and, over the front entrance, a restaurant. The Public Room became a cinema from May 1919, followed by the Majestic in Newnham Street in August 1933, advertised the next year as 'Ely's Cosy Cinema'. This was the first to close, 1959, but the building was soon in use again and is now a snooker hall. The Public Room, officially known as the Exchange Cinema from 1958, showed its last film on 13 May 1963, the Rex in January 1981; both are now demolished. A film club then showed films to its members and, from September 1987, a part-time cinema was opened at the Maltings. The Public Room had earlier been used for dances and, in 1910, a maple floor was installed so the hall could be used for roller skating. Until the large cinemascope screen was permanently in position c1953, the Rex Cinema had other uses; concerts, theatricals, operas, pantomimes and school prize-givings were held there.

Ely Horticultural Society held its first show of flowers, fruit and vegetables in the garden of the Bishop's Palace under 'the rich foliage of the majestic trees' on 19 May 1857. Later shows have been held there and elsewhere, including Paradise and the Maltings. Allotments have been popular for many years, particularly since World War I, and are still worked by keen gardeners at Barton Farm, Bridge Fen, Deacon's Lane, New Barns and Upherd's Lane.

Today, as the City becomes a tourist centre, there are many places where visitors and residents can relax over a meal. The Lamb Hotel remains the City's chief hotel, while restaurants include both Indian and Chinese as well as those serving traditional English food. Notable in that category is Old Fire Engine House which, combined with an Art Gallery, opened in 1968. The first artist to exhibit was fenland painter Anthony Day, who has held over 21 shows there. Many other artists and craftsmen continue to show amateur and professional work there and elsewhere in the City.

ABOVE: Hoop Trundling: in the distance is the monastic barn. (CEN) LEFT: John Titterton drew this c1870 and wrote 'The two ladies on the right were supposed to be "gone" on the parson. Just above his right hand is "Turkey" Smart the champion of his day, a quick but ungraceful skater with a gait like a turkey'. (CW) RIGHT: Cambridge University Crew: in the background is Steward's Malting, once owned by the Stuntney family during the early 17th century. The Cutter Inn next door was not licensed until c1830 when Sandy's Cut, a channel linking Ely directly to Littleport, was completed; the inn took its name from this cut.

ABOVE: The *Viscountess Bury,* built 1888, was chartered by Edward VII when Prince of Wales, and later based in Cambridge for some 60 years. Recently refitted, it is often moored near 'Carmuckill' Bridge. (CC) CENTRE: The *Pattie,* used for many years by fishing parties, is no longer on the river. During World War I she retrieved a crashed aircraft from the fen. The cup on 28 August 1910 was won by well-known angler, Arthur Meadows, a hairdresser in Broad Street. BELOW: Ladies were keen anglers too; here on 9 July 1929 near Ely High Bridge; Harry Meadows is in the centre with his son Arthur to his left.

ABOVE: Ely River Trip Society Committee, August 1909: a Tom Bolton photo, taken at the back of Cross's Tearooms where this rustic shelter, decorated with bark and mirrors, was sometimes used in summer. The PSA, Pleasant Sunday Afternoon, linked with the Countess of Huntingdon Chapel, was another group active then. LEFT: 'Caught by Arthur Newman, Ely 2 hours fishing, July 13 1911 weight 2 stone 1½ pounds.' The fish are bream. RIGHT: The Rex Cinema had many uses other than the showing of films — amateur and professional dramatics, concerts and school prize-givings until a cinemascope screen was installed c1953. (CC)

ABOVE: Ely Operatic Society on 29 April 1919 in *H.M.S. Pinafore:* W. Cobb is in the centre with (right) Gladys Woolnough. She had been a pupil at Ely High School when it opened in 1905 and lived into the 1980s. BELOW: Marshall Fisher is surrounded by the varied contents of his museum. He was once clerk to solicitor William Marshall and later to Evans and Sons who, for some 50 years, had premises in High Street Passage (EM)

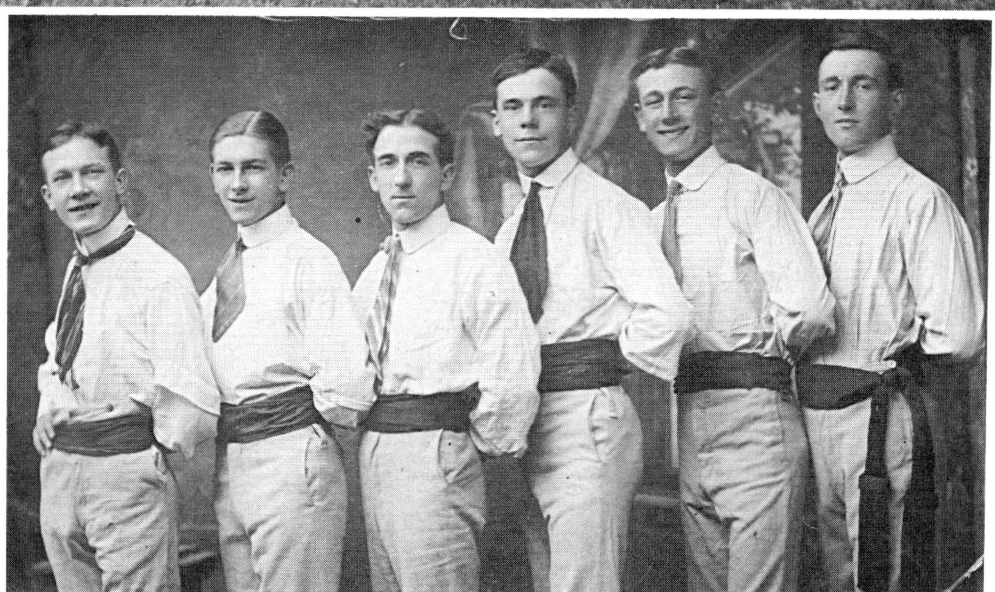

ABOVE: Ely Sports Association Committee c1893: left of the central figure is T. Blakeman, to the right Dr. H.H. Hulbert (who once lived at the Grange, now part of ECDC offices) with his infant son Jack, who became a well-known actor; centre front is Major Frank Roberson and R. Buckle, Treasurer 1893-1948, stands in the back row (second from left). BELOW: The Dandies c1913.

126 City of Ely Red Book.

FORE HILL, ELY.

Ye Olde Tea Rooms and Museum

THE ONLY MUSEUM IN THE CITY.

Has been visited by thousands, and praised by all.

Nothing like it for miles around.

All our Cakes, Pastry, and Biscuits are made in our own Bakery. Fresh daily.

Rustic Tea Garden

OPEN DURING SUMMER MONTHS.

Accommodation for 200.

Mrs. FRED. T. CROSS

Proprietress.

LEFT: Thought to date from the 16th century, F.T. Cross's Tea Rooms and Museum is now part of the Royal Standard. RIGHT: An advertisement from a City of Ely *Red Book,* a local directory of 1914, when Vernon's mother was in charge. BELOW: The interior of Ye Olde Tea Rooms and Museum: F.T. Cross began an 'Eating House' here in 1903; the exhibits which formed the museum gradually grew in number.

The Path of Usefulness

Learning and education in Ely probably began in the monastery. Henry Gunning reminisces: 'In the earliest days of English Benedictine monasticism it was customary for boys to be offered by their parents as oblates [recruits] to the cloister at a very early age, and this, it seems, is how the future King Edward the Confessor was brought to Ely by his parents'. This would have been c1006 and here, we are told, he joined 'in singing Psalms and Godly Hymns in the Cloister'. It is said that 'his unhappy brother, Alfred, ended his life a prisoner at Ely after his eyes had been put out by command of King Harold . . .'. The practice of admitting young boys ceased during the 12th century, but provision was made for educating the novices and 'there was also a school in the almonry' for poor boys who 'were housed, clothed, fed and taught' there. An Ely Grammar School certainly existed in the mid-15th century, for it is recorded that John Downham was appointed Master to 'to teach grammar within the Grammar School and nowhere else' and to take a number of services each week. At the time there was also a school for those who, taught by the Precentor, sang in the Lady Chapel.

The year 1541 was an important one for local education as statutes, confirmed in the following year, were issued for the Cathedral Grammar School to be funded by the new foundation. Only boys who could read and had some knowledge of grammar were admitted. Twenty-four poor boys, some probably children of the clergy, stayed at the school until they could speak Latin and write both Latin and Greek. Gradually the curriculum widened, but it still centred on the Classics. So began the school which became known as the King's School.

The School's numbers and achievements have varied but the period shortly before 1600 'might well claim to represent the golden age' when a great number of the 'paying pupils' as opposed to the 'King's Scolars' went on to the University of Cambridge. A particularly low ebb coincided with the headmastership of William Pamplyn, the quality of whose teaching was in doubt. In addition, his daughter lived in part of the school with the boarders and was suspected of 'very loose' behaviour. The school was 'made a dauncinge schoole' at night and her presence led to much that was unsatisfactory. The Dean, Dr Tyndall, dismissed Pamplyn in 1609. However the school survived both this and the Commonwealth period and continued into the present century. From 1858 to 1947 the Choir School was a separate establishment, with its own headmaster, and occupied part of the building to the west of Sacrist's Gate.

Housed in the Porta after the Reformation, the number of buildings used by the King's School has grown enormously since the Second World War, until today boarders are accommodated in School House (the range of monastic buildings situated in The Gallery), Walsingham House, the Priory, the Canonry, St Etheldreda House at the top of Back Hill, Old Hereward Hall and in St Mary's Street at number 24 and at the Choir School House. Offices are housed in the former Theological College, art studios in the Porta and a section of the monastic barn used by the school since 1922 has been converted into a superb dining-hall. Part of the former Barton Farm now belongs to the school and here there is a heated swimming pool and also new buildings for the Junior School (nine – 13 year olds). There are extensive playing fields, including Amherst Field on Bridge Road, donated by a former master, Miles Amherst.

Marion Saunders opened her school on Back Hill in 1949 but after one term moved to Acremont House in Egremont Street. This was for junior children until, when Audrey Cross, who had a school at 20 Chapel Street, became ill, Mrs Saunders took in her infants. Miss Cross did not recover, so the two schools became one in 1976. The infants' school had opened, probably about 1930 in Chapel Street. Then it seems that it was moved elsewhere in the city before returning to Chapel Street later in the 1930s where a Nissen hut, which remains today, provided a schoolroom behind the house. When Marion Saunders retired in 1982 the school remained at Acremont House but became part of the King's School under Headmistress Patricia Seekings. The King's School can therefore claim to be an independent co-educational school for boys and girls aged four to 18.

Shortly after Headmaster Hubert Ward was appointed in January 1970 two performances of a pageant, *A Thousand Ages in Thy Sight*, and a special service in the Cathedral commemorated the date when the monks 'a century after the Danish havoc . . . restored a tradition of education' in Ely. The mid-1940s began a period of expansion which continues. Girls were admitted in September 1970 and, on her first visit, the Queen recommended that up to 12 girls be appointed annually as Queen's Scholars to complement the King's Scholars created by Henry VIII. Numbers in the whole school, including both the Juniors and Infants in the 1990 Lent term, were 256 boarders and 568 day scholars; more than ever before.

Grammar school education for boys, partly catered for by the King's School, was also provided by nearby Soham Grammar School, whose foundation goes back to 1686, though probably no Ely boy was accepted before 1885 during the headship of W.H. Mould. Grammar school education for girls did not officially begin until 18 May 1905, when the High School for Girls opened its doors to generations of local children from the City and the nearby fenland area at Bedford House. 'The school at that time was contained in the main building, which left a lovely stretch of garden going right back to Chapel Street' but over the years it expanded to fill most of the space. A preparatory department for boys and girls opened in 1905, closely followed by the Kindergarten. This part of the school was forced to close in 1948 as a result of the 1944 Education Act. The High School for Girls moved to new buildings in Downham Road, opened by the Duchess of Gloucester in 1957. The school flourished under its four headmistresses, Miss E.E. Fletcher, Miss E.M. Verini, Dr Bertha Tilly and Miss E. Moody until 1972. Then it was absorbed into the City of Ely College, a comprehensive which was for a while one of a federation, with schools at Soham, Witchford and Littleport under Principal Peter Thacker. By September 1986 any idea of a federation had been abandoned and the City of Ely Community College, under Roger Daw, came into being.

Among early schools in Ely was one held in a building on the corner of Silver Street and The Gallery. Among the correspondence of Bishop Turner in the Bodleian Library is a letter from Robert Mingay, 17 January 1686; he tells of a Feoffees' meeting and the plans for a school which 'we are resolved shall be like the Hospitall Children of X's Ch'. The building, leased from Dr Hitch, was also to accommodate a House of Correction and a bridewell. It was a school for both boys and girls, since proposals for the regulation of the House of Correction stated that the Master and his wife were to be 'Governing teaching washing and looking after . . . all poore children and Orphans . . . of whatever age or sex soever'. When the lease terminated in 1696, the building ceased to be used for these purposes. Much later, in the 19th century, poor children were given some education at the Union.

In 1813 the Dean and Chapter granted a large room 'within the Precincts of the Cathedral' for use as a school for 200 boys; a year later the Girls' Day School was accommodated in a room over the Sessions House on the Market Place. The girls moved in 1820 to a new Junior School in Market Street and by 1859 National Schools at Broad Street and Silver Street had been built for infants and older girls respectively.

In 1933 the school in Market Street, which had been rebuilt in 1868 for £430, became a Mixed Infants' School; this closed after St Audrey's School opened in 1953 on Downham Road. St Audrey's building, now used as a Sixth Form Centre, closed for infants in 1985, when all children of that age transferred to the newly named County Infants' School. This, previously known as St Etheldreda's School, had opened on the High Barns campus in 1973. The Broad Street school also changed status in 1933, from an infants to a junior girls' school.

Boys of seven to 14 years had had the choice up to then of two schools; Needham's and the National School at Silver Street. The younger boys, under Headmaster Fred Thrower, were then transferred to Silver Street, where older girls were already, and Needham's became a school for senior boys. In 1961 St Mary's Church of England Junior Mixed School was formed, housed at Silver Street and Broad Street. The Broad Street school closed in 1968, by which time it was used by only one class, and the other classes transferred to Silver Street. Soon after this the Broad Street building was converted for use by Ely Pottery. This too closed and was later gutted by fire in 1981, and subsequently demolished. The Junior Mixed School moved to Bedford House in 1968 and remained there until new premises were ready at High Barns; that school was officially opened on 20 October 1971.

Needham's School was established in 1740 following Catherine Needham's will; money for clothing and education was provided. From the next year, reading, writing and arithmetic were taught to 24 boys, who were also given a suit of clothing each year. The Free School, as it was known, required some boys to pay a few pence per week; by 1903, when the school was considerably enlarged, 75% of the boys who attended paid sixpence per week. The first Headmaster was William Cawthorne the Younger, whose sister Mary married Morley Unwin. She and her husband were friendly with poet William Cowper, who is said to have written several poems to her, including the sonnet which begins 'Mary! I want a lute with other strings'. Apprenticeship of poor boys of the City was also accommodated. In the 19th century more than half were bound to trades in Ely, a minority went as far as Boston, Grantham and London. Up to 1933 there was also a Boys' National School in Silver Street for the same age group: seven - 14 years. The school's status changed in 1933 and it then took in Ely boys from 11 years and was known as Ely Needham's Senior Boys' School; junior boys were housed in the north side of the Silver Street School. As a result of the 1944 Education Act there was further change – the school became Ely Needham's Secondary Modern Boys' School. In 1969, the school building on Back Hill became a Teachers' Centre and is now a County Council Technology Centre.

After the 1944 Act Needham's Girls' School, senior girls, continued at Silver Street in the part nearest to the Range until, after the completion of new buildings for the High School for Girls in 1957, they moved with Headmistress Elsie Seymour to Bedford House. The Silver Street buildings were demolished c1970 to make way for houses. On Miss Seymour's retirement, the Needham's boys moved from Back Hill to Bedford House and the school became a Mixed Secondary Modern School under Headmaster Tom Walker. These premises were used for about ten years until 1968, when new buildings on the Downham Road campus were opened in September. This school, with the Girls' High School, became part of a comprehensive school in 1972.

There were also evening classes, lectures, the Mechanics' Institute, small private schools and Sunday Schools. In the Ely diocese the 'rural deans had made returns about the number of schools in 1782 – and very few there were . . .'. In about 1786 'activity began' when Caesar Morgan at Ely was asked to raise a subscription for a Sunday School; the Bishop 'would contribute five guineas and the wages of a dame'. Morgan said that 'Sunday Schools promising. I attend one or more of them every Sunday and have heard most of them say the Lord's prayer. I shall next proceed to the Creed and so on to the ten commandments'. At Holy Trinity some pupils needed correction by sidesmen who 'equipped with a useful wand, had a "down" on the Sunday School boys sitting at the back of the church who were APT TO BE RESTIVE . . .'.

Evening classes were opened for members of the Militia by Rev W. Selwyn in 1852 for 'giving lectures and instructing such soldiers that liked to attend, in reading, writing and arithmetic'. The Dean and Chapter lent a room and the classes were 'under superintendence of Mr Pountney and his son; masters of Mrs Needham's Free School'. Students were carefully assessed and study arranged to lead them 'gently along in the path of usefulness and duty both temporal and spiritual . . . It is a praiseworthy arrangement, and we have no doubt of its successful operation'. During the middle of the 19th century these classes were attended by between 150 and 200 students and continued until at least 1861. Evening classes flourished, particularly post-World War II to 1986, when a great variety of classes were held at Bedford House.

Sunday Schools were also considered in 1813 at a meeting convened by the Lord Bishop for 'the promotion of Education in the Doctrine and Discipline of the established Religion . . .'. This was attended by notable citizens of the time: Francis Bagge Esq, Chief Bailiff of the Isle of Ely, Thomas Page, occupant of Bedford House, Jonathan Page of Cromwell House, William Apsey, James Golborne, Mr Robert Muriel, surgeon, Thomas Spooner, Seth Bull, Mr Henry Martin, Mr Charles Bidwell, who was responsible for the 1851 map of Ely, Mr Thomas Archer, and solicitor Mr H.R. Evans. At a later meeting a great many resolutions were approved, including one 'That the Children do meet in the School-Room every Sunday Morning at half-past Eight, and every Sunday Afternoon at half-past One; and proceed from thence regularly and orderly to Divine Service . . .'. A subscription list was opened and contains names of many citizens, including tradesmen. Boys do not change: it was resolved 7 November 1814 that 'refractory Boys' should be removed from the school, that 'a Black Hole be prepared for the Correction of naughty boys', and that 'the Master should repeat his injunctions to the Boys respecting the pernicious habit, now so prevalent, of throwing stones'. Today Sunday Schools at St Mary's, the Cathedral and the chapels attract considerable numbers.

Apart from these official establishments there were many small, privately run schools. In 1798 three or four small schools were kept by women. In 1814 Miss Sarah and Miss Elizabeth Muriel were preparing to open a Boarding and Day School for Young Ladies. They had taken a large house; 'having spent several years in London, they flatter themselves that their plan of Education will meet with the "approbation and encouragement of their friends"'. In the 1820s the Misses Doswell had a school in High Row (High Street) where young ladies could board and have tuition. For many years Mr and Mrs Trigg advertised their school, which opened in 1828 somewhere in the College, after they had taken over Mr Scott's Mathematical and Commercial School. At first their school was advertised as a 'Classical and Commercial School', later as an 'Academy'. Situated in Fore Hill by 1852, there were 34 boarders and 21 day scholars. Pupils at Miss Briggs' school or 'Ladies Seminary' were 'expected to curtsy on entering the schoolroom and to leave the same with a profound bow. Manners of repose were inculcated, and "TOO MUCH FRIVOLITY in the hall" was promptly denounced'.

The list of scholastic establishments for a small city seems unending; since the last war, Larkfield Adult Training Centre and Highfield, a 'special' school, have opened, the Red Cross School in the former Bishop's Palace has opened and closed and the English College for overseas students in Waterside was started in 1978 by Barbara Eaton. The Theological College, 'The Theo' as it was known, founded in 1876, opened in 1881 for 20 students in buildings on Barton Square, now used by the King's School. With the exception of two wartime periods, the College remained open until 1964 when, under Principal Canon Douglas Hill, it was closed 'temporarily' and the bell, whose sound had marked the hours between Prime at 7.00 am and Compline at 9.30 pm, ceased to ring. In the grounds, Bishop Woodford House, a retreat and conference centre with a new Diocesan Office attached, was built in 1969.

Then there are libraries and Reading Rooms. A library of nearly 2,000 volumes was at the Mechanics' Institute which opened in 1842. The City of Ely Institute and Reading Room was at Naverino House, now Kempton's, on Fore Hill. Also there have been various small subscription libraries, for example at Bird's and at Burrows' in High Street and at Oakey's in St Mary's Street, where books, mostly fiction, could be borrowed during this century. The first branch of the County Library opened in the 1940s in Bray's Lane, where solicitor Martin Hall's house and garden had been. On the corner of the Palace Green, where there was once a second Cross's Tea Room, an Ely Branch Library opened in new purpose-built premises on 5 April 1966. The building gained a Civic Trust Award and is often considered the only modern building in Ely with any claim to distinction.

Reports of lectures in the local press of this and the last century were frequent; subjects ranged from What is Man?, Astronomy, Public Health and Christian Catacombs of Rome, illustrated with lantern slides ('warmly received'), to Black Magic and Witchcraft. Today many societies exist which have a regular programme of lectures and talks on equally wide-ranging subjects.

A group of King's School boys standing just inside the Porta, with the gable end of the Queen's Hall in front of the west tower.

One way
FREE
CAR PARK

OPPOSITE ABOVE: 1882: left is a building on the site of Canon Hitch's house, part of which was later used as a school and then as the Green Man. The lamp-post said by students of the Theological College in the words of the hymn to be: 'A light to shine upon the road That leads me to the Lamb,' was on their route to the Lamb Hotel. LEFT: Needham's School on Back Hill, built 1740. (BL) RIGHT: The Theological College: in the niche on the south wall is a statue of the founder Bishop Woodford. (CC) BELOW: The northern wing of the Silver Street School with the teacher's house, between the two wings just before demolition. Two houses now stand on there. ABOVE: 'The Dairy Class' at the back of the Silver Street building c1923. Headmistress Miss Knights (centre); (left-right): Marjorie Aveling, Ivy Cross, Gert Oakey, Olive Lane, Emily Crouch, Doris Negus, Mabel Martin, Dorothy Thompson, Kate Westley and Kathleen Ablett. BELOW: The Broad Street School after the fire 1981.

Other Ways

In 1457 three Lollards, or followers of Wycliff, were brought before the Bishop because they had attacked the church for its worldliness and corruption. None of the three were Ely men but, after Bishop William Grey pronounced them suspect of heresy, each agreed to perform any penance imposed, part of which in this instance was to walk round Ely Market Place 'clad only in shirt and trousers, with a faggot on his back and a 1d wax candle in his hand . . .'. After that each asked for 'Forgyvenes of there opinions errour and heresies above said and grace of the holy ghost' that he 'falle no more in to these nor noon othre errours in tyme comyng'.

The 'Ely Martyrs', William Wolsey and Robert Pygot, both Wisbech men, were accused of the particular heresy of not believing that the body and blood of Christ were present in the bread and wine of the sacrament of mass. They were pronounced guilty and declared 'heretic and excommunicate'. They were burnt at the stake on 16 October 1555, probably on the Palace Green in front of Ely Cathedral. In this century the Protestant Alliance mark the event by an annual service held on the Monday nearest to the date of the martyrdom. Permission was not given for the erection of a memorial on the Green.

There was apparently little Protestant Dissent in the early days following the Reformation, as was perhaps to be expected 'in a city so literally overshadowed by its cathedral as was Ely'. In 1676, four years after the Declaration of Indulgence, 'only 33 Protestant Nonconformists and one Papist were reported'.

Almost a century later, John Wesley visited Ely in November 1774 and preached in 'a house well filled with plain, loving people' and so, in a sense, founded the Ely Methodist Church. However, the first mention of the Ely Methodists occurs in 1807 in the Bishop's Visitation Records. At that time there were few Methodists in Trinity Parish but in St Mary's there was a Methodist meeting house 'supposed to be licenced'. In 1808 the Ely Methodist Society applied for and obtained from the Bishop a licence to hold religious meetings at a house in Harlock's Lane, now Back Lane, in Trinity Parish; there was also a Sunday School. When the Methodists moved in December 1811 to premises on Fore Hill, Thomas (a cordwainer) and Rebecca Kempton were signatories to the request for a licence. After about four months the group moved to 48 St Mary's Street: the minister lived next door in the small cottage to the east of the house; the chapel was at the back, through the archway that is still there.

A site was obtained in Chapel Street where the new chapel opened on 30 December 1818; there was preaching morning, afternoon and evening that day. A few years later, due to changes within the Methodist movement, this became known as the Wesleyan Chapel. Although it had

ABOVE: The back of Bedford House after the 1920 extension (right), now removed, had been added. On the left are the kindergarten and preparatory classrooms, now demolished. CENTRE: Ely High School Form Vb, Easter Term 1915, in the gymnasium, then in the front of the building where the floor had been specially lowered. BELOW: At the back of Bedford House in 1986, shortly before all the huts were demolished: the Cambridgeshire Housing Society has now built new accommodation there. On the left is the former assembly hall and on the far right the former laboratory.

already been enlarged it soon proved too small and was demolished to make way for a larger chapel with a schoolroom behind. Richard Freeman was employed; he was a well-known local builder who, in the 1850s, had built the small cottage on Barton Road for £100. 15 September 1858 saw the official opening of the 'House of God' which, unlike the earlier building, faced onto Chapel Street and was said to hold 600. Since then the schoolroom has been enlarged and, in 1891, when the original front became dangerous, a new facade of red brick with stone facings was constructed. At the beginning of the 20th century the interior was completely renovated and modernised. When enlarged accommodation to the rear was opened in 1920, built on donated land, festivities lasted for two days and included services, a luncheon, an organ recital by Noel Ponsonby, Cathedral organist, and an evening rally attended by guests from other denominations. Many local people have been associated with the chapel, including Philip Tow, fishmonger, Alfred Williamson, grocer, Henry Morgan, painter and decorator, James Eusden, brickmaker and builder, members of the Lemon, Shillaker, Ablett, Holland and Tucker families.

The Primitive Methodists, a breakaway group, established in Ely in the 1830s, built a chapel in 1847 in Victoria Street (then New Street). By 1885 it had to be enlarged; at the same time a schoolroom was built and a minister's house next door to the chapel. In 1932 the Deed of Union was signed, so in Ely the Wesleyans and the Primitive Methodists united and this was marked by a three day long celebration. The union led to the eventual redundancy of the Victoria Street building; c1962 a small factory opened there and remained for about 20 years.

The Countess of Huntingdon chapel, built on its present site in Chapel Street probably in 1793, is a typical 'meeting house' building. It was closed for a short time at the end of the 18th century but re-opened in 1802 and increased in strength until 1851, 'when there were over 400 adult worshippers and 200 Sunday scholars . . . the largest congregation in the city'. The interior was refurbished in 1985.

When one group left the Countess of Huntingdon congregation a Salem chapel was built in 1840 in Chequer Lane and used by the Independent Baptists until about 1875. In 1853 or earlier, the Strict Baptist Church built the Zion Chapel in Butcher's Row (the site of mediaeval butchers' shops) between High Street and Market Street. About 40 years ago the congregation numbered around 25; today it is about a quarter of that. The chapel has no permanent minister but sometimes services are taken by visiting ministers. The building, which belongs to the Strict Baptist Trust, is thought to have original panelling inside and to have been little altered. The Salem Chapel was used for a time by the Church of England Men's Society, probably after it had been bought by Thomas Cropley for £160 (contents for £6). Later it was sold to the Ely and District Liberal Club for £250; it is now used as a store.

After the Reformation the Catholic community in Cambridgeshire did not build a church until 1840; this was at Wisbech and was shortly followed by one in Cambridge. Here Canon Quinlivan was in charge and, after July 1845 when the Cambridge to Norwich railway opened, made many visits to Ely where he celebrated mass in a private house. Later, a member of the Jesuit Fathers travelled to Ely from Newmarket and in 1889 celebrated mass at a Mr Fischer's on Forehill. In 1890 Father Freeland, with £10 and his Bishop's blessing came 'to establish a new parish' in Ely. He eventually rented a room in Market Street and provided for a congregation of about 16, until a simple corrugated iron building was erected on land purchased in Egremont Street 1892. By then the congregation had grown to about 40 and included Arthur Harvey, brewery worker, who was baptised at about 30 years of age and served at Sunday mass for 50 years until his death in 1948.

A more suitable building became essential; £100 was donated by a newcomer to the City and was followed by an appeal. After five or six years 'the Old Iron Church' was replaced and a presbytery built. The official opening of the Church of St Etheldreda took place on 17 October 1903 on the Feast of St Etheldreda's Translation, when the church was blessed by Bishop Riddell, who then celebrated a 'Pontifical High Mass' in the presence of some 40 priests. A luncheon was provided by the Lamb Hotel and served in the Public Room. Meanwhile Arthur Brunning, members of whose family still faithfully serve the church, had by 1903 moved to Ely and a number of converts had been received, one of whom was Richard Toombs, last of five generations of barbers of that name in the City. The Beet Sugar Factory, opened 1925, attracted a number of Irish workers whose presence swelled the congregation. In the early 1930s members of the Harvey family became benefactors and later builder Henry Wykes, who had been a cathedral lay clerk, joined the group.

The war opened the way for pastoral work, still carried on today, at the RAF Hospital and the congregation was swelled by 'temporary residents', Germans and Italians, from the prisoner of war camp in Barton Fields on Cambridge Road. When Father Pritchard was inducted in 1947, Germans, Rumanians and Poles, the latter from the Resettlement Camp at Chippenham, were present. Bishop Iwan Buzko came in 1948 to meet Ukranian Displaced Persons from the camps in the area, including the camp at Ely on West Fen Road. A number of these men married local girls who were not of the Catholic faith. This led to a great many catechism classes, conducted by Miss Mallylon Thompson and Miss Lilian Brunning, both still members of the church.

The 50th anniversary of the opening of the building held in 1953 was marked by the return of a relic of St Etheldreda, her left hand, to Ely; it is enshrined behind a glass screen in the north aisle. Over the years, various changes have been made to the interior; Miss Dorothy Defew provided in her will for a number of improvements, carried out in preparation for the long-awaited dedication on 22 May 1987.

There are apparently few references to Quakers in Ely before this century, though a John Tubbs who died in January 1795 was 'one of the people called quakers; a punctual, honest man'. From 4 March 1979 a group of Friends met at 23 Fore Hill, Ely and continued to do so until 1981, when the Meeting moved to Stretham. In 1982 the first Recognised Meeting was held at the Old Palace School and, after a break of about one year, continued at Stretham and now at Witcham Methodist Chapel.

The Salvation Army began its work in Ely in the 1890s in premises in Victoria Street referred to in 1893 as 'Salvation Army Barracks'. Although the building continued in the ownership of the Army, it was used for other purposes, including a gymnasium, before it was re-opened with new furnishings and fittings in 1934. It finally closed as Army quarters in 1939 and during the war was used by the Sea Cadet Corps.

Still used by the Railway Mission, their hall in Silver Street was built in 1901 for use by a group who had previously met in the 'Waiting Room up platform – Sunday Afternoon 2.30 pm'.

The Ely Christian Fellowship, formed in 1982, at first held meetings at the Ely Maltings, but now holds them at the Larkfield Centre. Another group of Christians who have met together since 1958, at first in premises at Market Street have, since October 1985, met in the Gospel Hall at Ship Lane, in a building once used as an additional classroom at the Broad Street School.

'The Martyrdom of W. Wolsey & R. Pygot at Ely.' This has been printed backwards the better to show that the martyrdom may have taken place on the Palace Green. (CEN)

LEFT: The Countess of Huntingdon Chapel, Chapel Street. (BL) RIGHT: The Zion Chapel, Butcher's Row. (BL) BELOW: A print of the Methodist Chapel, Chapel Street as it appeared in 1859. (DM)

ABOVE: The Church of England Working Men's Society Ely Branch, c1890, gathered outside their hall, built as a Salem Chapel. BELOW: Interior of St Etheldreda's Roman Catholic Church in Egremont Street, c1930.

ABOVE: Three gentlemen on the Market Place about, their newspaper suggests, to spread 'The Joyful News'. BELOW: Church Congress 1910, when the progress of the procession along High Street was recorded by a succession of photos taken by Tom Bolton.

Ely Cathedral: a great building and house of prayer, which dominates the City today as it has done for over eight hundred year

Look Foward

Today Ely is on the brink of more change than for many years, perhaps for centuries. Leaving aside the question of whether or not the warming of the earth and the raising of the sea level leads to Ely once again becoming an island, the inevitable rise in the East Anglian population will certainly bring change. There is considerable pressure to develop new villages and towns not only near Ely, but throughout East Anglia; this will have an affect on the City. Predictably, before many years have passed, the City itself will expand within the boundaries provided by the river and, since 1986, the by-pass. The electrification of the railway line from London to King's Lynn will open the area to the south and, with the completion of the Channel Tunnel, to Europe. Major improvements to the A10 road, which links Ely to Cambridge, will encourage this development.

The City centre will change too when the proposed new shopping area to the north of the Market Place is developed. This will be welcomed by many, but others will mourn the loss of the Thursday meeting-place and of the auctions held in this former Cattle Market. Nevertheless, much of the heart of Ely will remain; the street plan has altered little since mediaeval days and, although shops and offices come and go, many buildings survive. If, for example, you look up beyond street level in the High Street and inside the buildings and behind them you will see part of Ely's past.

The most important link with this past is the magnificant Cathedral and, due to the initiative of the Dean and Chapter, much has already been done to conserve and restore both the Cathedral and the monastic buildings. The Lady Chapel has recently re-opened, the scaffolding from the east end and the south transept has been taken down, but elsewhere work continues. A 21st Century Fund has been set up so that, as far as is possible, the Cathedral shall never again lack the finance to ensure its preservation.

For those with eyes to see, the past is certainly visible in this City and many now appreciate its long and interesting development. It is to be hoped that, in spite of inevitable change and growth, the essential character of Ely will be safeguarded in future years.

Internal work was carried out in the Lady Chapel 1939 but after that little work was done before 1951. This list provides a summary of the main work carried out since then with the approximate dates.

1951-53	Octagon and lantern; work carried out to eliminate death watch beetle. Leadwork repaired and octagon timbers strengthened.
1953	Choir roof releaded.
1955	Lantern roof releaded.
1955-63	South and north transept roofs releaded.
1956	Nave roof; some work carried out to eliminate death watch beetle.
1958-59	North choir; partly roofed with copper.
1959	Octagon leadwork repaired.
1959-60	South choir aisle roof repaired.
1964	Choir vestry re-roofed. Galilee Porch stonework repaired.
1962-64	South-west transept roof repaired.
1965	Presbytery triforium windows glazed with clear glass.
1970	Lady Chapel; window tracery repaired.
1971-72	West tower strengthened and repaired.
1975	Organ rebuilt.
1978	Lady Chapel north side pinnacles repaired.
1980-81	Galilee Porch; roof repaired.
1982	Choir vault repaired.
1987	Nave and north nave aisle roofs, work begun.
1987-88	Nave; painted ceiling cleaned and restored.
1988-90	Lady Chapel; re-roofed, high level stonework repaired, windows below tracery strengthened and reglazed, new lighting installed. East end; stonework repaired. North choir aisle; two bays restored.
1989-90	South transepts; structural work carried out and stonework repaired.
1990	Lantern windows; repair started.

Sources & Bibliography

Original Sources

Many records are available at the Cambridgeshire Collection, Cambridge Central Library, the County Record Office and the University Library, Cambridge; records are also to be found in national collections and in the archives of local charities and other organisations in Ely. Further material collected by the late Reg Holmes is available for the use of researchers.

Catalogues of Resource Material

Gibbons, A. *Ely Episcopal Records* (1891)
Owen, Dorothy *A Catalogue of the Records of the Bishop and Archdeacon of Ely* (1971)
——, *The Muniments of Ely Cathedral Priory* (1976)

Printed Sources

Dring, W.E. *The Fen and the Furrow* (1974)
Petty, Michael *The Cambridgeshire Collection An annotated catalogue of the books and periodicals acquired 1855–1983.* This is an introduction to accompany fiche catalogue.

Select Bibliography

Archer, Goodwyn L. *Old Ely, Cambridgeshire* (1949)
Astbury, A.K. *The Black Fens* (1958)
Atkinson, Thomas Dinham *An Architectural History of the Benedictine Monastery of St Etheldreda at Ely* (1933)
Beckett, John *The Urgent Hour* (1974)
Bede *A History of the English Church and People* (Sherley-Price 1955)
Bentham, James *The History and Antiquities of the Conventual and Cathedral Church of Ely* (1771, and with supplement 1812)
Blake, E.O. edit *Liber Eliensis* (1962)
Chapman, F.R. edit *Sacrist Rolls of Ely Volume One Notes on Transcripts* (1907)
——, *Sacrist Rolls of Ely Volume Two Transcripts* (1907)
Clements, J.H. *A Brief History of The City of Ely and Neighbouring Villages in The Isle* (1868)
Cobb, Gerald *English Cathedrals The Forgotten Centuries* (1980)
Coldstream and Draper, edit *The British Archaeological Association Conference Transactions for the Year 1976 II Medieval Art and Architecture at Ely Cathedral* (1979)
Darby, H.C. *The Draining of the Fens* (1940)
——, *The Medieval Fenland* (1940)
——, *The Changing Fenland* (1983)
Dorman, Bernard *The Story of Ely and Its Cathedral* (1968)
Dugdale, W. *The History of Imbanking and Drayning of Divers Fens and Marshes* (1662)
Goodwin, Harvey *Ely Gossip* (1892)
Holmes, Reg *That Alarming Malady* (1974)
——, *Cromwell's Ely* (1975)
——, *Ely Inns* (1984)
Holton-Krayenbuhl, Ann *The Three Blackbirds: a medieval house in Ely* (1984)
Ladds, S. Inskip *The Monastery at Ely* (1930)
Lee, William *Report to the General Board of Health* (1850)
Mason, H.J. *The Black Fens* (1973)
Merivale, Charles *St Etheldreda Festival. Summary of Proceedings* (1873)
Miller, E. *The Abbey and Bishopric of Ely* (1951)
Miller, Samuel H. and Skertchley, Sydney, B.J. *The Fenland Past and Present* (1878)
Morris, Christopher edit *The Journeys of Celia Fiennes* (1949)
Morris, John edit *Domesday Book 18 Cambridgeshire* (1981)
Owen, Dorothy and Thurley, Dorothy edit *The King's School, Ely* (1982)
Pevsner, Nikolaus *The Buildings of England Cambridgeshire* (1954)
Porter, Enid *Cambridgeshire Customs and Folklore* (1969)
——, *Proceedings of the Cambridge Antiquarian Society* (1865 onward)
Ravensdale, J.R. *Liable to Flood* (1974)
Rouse, M.R. *Ely in Old Picture Postcards* (1983)
Salzman, L.F. edit *The Victoria History of the Counties of England of Cambridge and the Isle of Ely Volume Two* (1948)
Saunders, W.H. Bernard and Sweeting, W.D. *Fenland Notes and Queries Volumes I to VII* (1889-1908)
Stewart, D.J. *On the Architectural History of Ely Cathedral* (1868)
Stubbs, Charles William *Ely Cathedral Handbook* (1906)
——, *Historical Memorials of Ely Cathedral* (1897)
Thorpe, B. edit *Anglo-Saxon Chronicle* (1861)
Zarnecki G. *The Early Sculpture of Ely* (1958)

Appendix

Business 1900–1990 in the Main Streets of Ely

(Not all 1930 businesses appear, only those trading in 1900 or 1990.)

ST MARY'S STREET

south side from west

1900, (1930 underlined)	1990, (1930 underlined)
Plough and Fleece (G. Ellis)	
White Lion (Mrs Jeffrey)	Covill's Cycle Centre
S. Coxon, surgeon dentist	OLIVER CROMWELL'S HOUSE
ST MARY'S CHURCH	ST MARY'S CHURCH
G. Comins, auctioneer	ELY DISPENSARY
E. Barnard, builder	The Ely Bookshop
ELY DISPENSARY	Ely Print Centre
Miss Clark, District Nurse	Ken Day Electrics
J. Cole, shoeing smith	(later William Brand blacksmith)
J. Rich, greengrocer	
W. Gotobed, Sutton's Parcels	(Lloyds Bank)

north side from west

1900, (1930 underlined)	1990, (1930 underlined)
J. Bickley, grocer	Snipetts
Mrs Larkins, butcher	Lemmon, butcher
Mrs Porter, builder	Tim Brinton Cars Ltd
G. Porter, tailor	Restaurant
Crown and Anchor	Ely Fish Bar
Mrs Beaumont	
G. Ashby, house decorator	Stephenson Davies, accountants
Arthur Allen, baker	
Electricity (offices)	
S.C. Harris, surgeon	
S. Pikett, butcher	
A. Hone, miller	
Sub PO Mrs Jefferson, stationer	
Jones & Jefferson, bookbinders	G. Ashby & Son
P. Chambers, carpenter	
W. Chambers, grocer	
G.J. Woolnough, provisions	Boden & Co
(DOWNHAM ROAD)	
G. Wycherley, glazer & decorator	Garden Gate Flowers
G. Sewell, wheelwright	BEDFORD HOUSE
Peacock Inn	Birch's Garage Ltd
J. Harle, bill poster	The Black Horse Agency
C. Bidwell, estate agent	King's Arms
Ed T. Pettit, baker	Gutteridge, hairdresser
A.J. Clifford, grocer	Marshall's of Ely, tobacconist
King's Arms (F.J. Cook)	D. Gibbs & Son
Mrs Macdonald, confectioner	Mrs Mills, antiques
Geo E. Legge, butcher	(1930 betw Gutteridge & Dobson
H. Dobson, hairdresser	was Thomas Coates tobacconist &
Rodwell Bros	Madame Coates, gowns, milliner)

HIGH STREET

north side from west

1900, (1930 underlined)	1990, (1930 underlined)
	Frank Peake, gents' outfitter
Pashler & Co, decorators	Burrows, newsagents
J. Gardiner, chemist	Ely Electrical Services
Legge & Son, bootmakers, shoes	Gibbs of Ely Ltd, shoes
A. Pledger, draper etc	Argos
A.D. Pledger, insurance agent	Gas
H. & J. Cutlack, ironmongers	Occasions, cards, gifts
(CHEQUER LANE)	Freeman, Hardy & Willis, shoes
Foster & Co, bankers	CHEQUER LANE
A. Davidson, clothier & draper	Bonnett's Café
Bell Hotel (J.C. Laxton)	Anglia Fruiterers
J. Home, wine & spirits	Currys
Miss Rope, china warehouse	Savory & Moore, chemist
J.M. Harvey, draper etc	Dewhursts, butchers
H.W. Gilbert, tailor etc	Ely Trophy Shop
(HIGH STREET PASSAGE)	American Express Travel Agents
(W.J. Evans, solicitor)	Sue Ryder Shop
O.J. Thurmott, harnessmaker	Bowgens, bakers
	United News Shops
	Oxfam
	HIGH STREET PASSAGE
Williamson & Dingle, grocers	Superdrugs
W. Lincolne, chemist	Paul Day, sports
Morriss' bazaar	Alliance Leicester, building society
J. Snell, draper	Peck's ironmongers
Geo Peck, ironmonger	Barries
William Ellis, draper	Peter Dominic
Dolphin (Jno Newstaed)	

south side from west

1900, (1930 underlined)	1990, (1930 underlined)
J.W. Rignall, photographer	The Prudential
H. Kempton & Co, tailors	Krystopha, hairdresser
T.P. Bendall, solicitor	Ritz Video Centre
F.M. Beckett, surgeon	Hall Enion & Young, solicitors
W. Crawley, harness maker	Fenway, TV, video
P. Chambers, pork butcher	2Ms, stationery, office equipment
GRAINGER'S PORCH	Ely Lighting & Gifts
Briggs, butcher	Job Centre

1900, (1930 underlined) 1990, (1930 underlined) 1900, (1930 underlined) 1990, (1930 underlined)
(Not all 1930 businesses appear, only those trading in 1900 or 1990.)

S.A. Cherer, pork pies
J. Barber, confectioner
Shelton & Tibbitts, printers
Arthur Northrop, butcher
Barclay & Company Ltd, bank

Mother Nature
Trustee Savings Bank
Steeple Gate, teashop, crafts
Olivers, shoes
M. Edis, butcher
Constance Wools
Barclays Bank
Jumpers
Cox Country Clothes
ELY MUSEUM
Ely Cathedral Shop

FORE HILL
south side from west

D. Goodin, tailor
A.W. Morris, clothier
E.S. Payne, tobacconist
Jno Gotobed, painter
Freeman, Hardy & Willis, shoes
Mrs Scott, earthenware dealer
Singer's, sewing machines
Joshua Taylor, clothier
F.T. Cross, baker etc
Royal Standard (J. Redhead)
Jas Prior, bootmaker
J.G. Benson, baker etc
Rose & Crown, (W. Bailey)
A.G. Sawyer, jeweller
Herbert Sykes, picture framer
T.W. Blakeman, currier
Mrs Bolton, photographer
Frederick Cope, tea merchant
Wm Gotobed, gardener
Thos Stocker, gardener
Mrs Hills, baker

The Woolwich, building society
Premier Travel Group
Wise Guy, fashions
Shoe Services
Smith's Cleaners
Your Price, fashions
Robert Hutchinson, optician
Woolworths
Reflections
City Hair Market
Brown & Co Ltd
Royal Standard
Peking Duck
Gallery Frames
City Kitchens
Alexandra House, music publishers

(1930 near top of hill was Maypole Dairy Co Cross's premises 1990 are part of The Royal Standard)

north side from west

Sturton & Howard, chemist
Eastman & Co Ltd, butchers
(City of Ely Inst & Read Rm)
General Supply Stores Co
J. Nightingale, eating house
Mrs Scott, basket maker
W. Robinson, architect
J.M. Evans, family butcher
T.R. Addison, solicitor
J. Rodgers, solicitor
J. Woodroffe, painter
Fisher & Co, furnishings
Constitutional Club
International Tea Stores
Charles Wood, gardener
A. & B. Hall, brewers
Round of Beef, (W. Newby)
Louis King, leather merchant
Clements & Son, printers
N. Coe, marine store
Maid's Head (J. Roberts)
George Fox, butcher

Highline Fashions
Wraggs, fancy goods
Dewhursts, butchers
Kemptons, fashions
Margarets, fashions
The Cromwell, restaurant
J.M. Evans, gents outfitters
Lynn Music
R. Milwright, vet
Courts, furnishings
Bennett's Bookshop
Cambridgeshire Philatic Auctions
Flemings Wines

(Freeman, Hardy & Willis remained on Fore Hill into the 1980s. Singer Co Ltd later became Green's, radio etc & is now the City Hair Market. 1930 Rayment, butcher is now Milwright's)

WATERSIDE
south side from west

W.H. Norman, basker maker
Queen's Head (W. Hall)
F.L. Harlock, brewer
W. Cross, corn merchant
Thos Bangley, baker
John Lee, dealer
Cooper's Arms (J. Dunham)
ALMSHOUSES
Chas Warner, tailor

(It is noticeable that during the 20th century the number of businesses has grown in Market Street but has reduced in number in St Mary's Street, Broad Street and Station Road)

north side from west

Mrs Cook, dressmaker
Black Bull, (B. Oakman)
H. Meadows, grocer
Three Crowns (Ellis King)
W. Bidwell, blacksmith
John Fear, basket maker
U D Surveyor's Office

Ely Boat Chandlers
Waterside Antiques
The English College
Precept Design Consultants
Archimage Architects/Designs

MARKET STREET
north side from west

W.G. Dunwoody, surgery
Infants' School
Watson Haylock, farmer
CATHOLIC PRESBYTERY
H.G. Martin, auctioneer
John Jefferson, butcher
F. Wilson, saddler
BUTTON'S YARD
Matthews & Co, watchmakers
Woolpack (W. Peacock)
Misses Bird, ladies school
Thos Legge, brewer

south side from west

Lamb Tap (Jno Mapson)
J.O. Vince, coach builder
J.P. Page, gasfitter
Miss Gleaves, dressmaker
Sun Inn (Jos Lawrence)
Matthews & Co, furnishers
F. Morley, shoemakers

F. Powell, stonemason
(HIGH STREET PASSAGE)
Surveyor of Taxes & Excise
Post Office
W.S. Kempton, upholster

MARKET PLACE

(1930 Bolton's Bazaar, Alfred E. Dean on south side, Thurmotts, leather, Fred Bennett, grocer & Rex Cinema north)
Empress of India, restaurant
Clipso, hairdresser
Ferrari's, restaurant
S & H Taxis
Chapman Harvey, printers
M E R, hairdresser
Hazy Days, fabrics
Carol Kennedy, fashions
Steve Spriggs, sports
Ely Standard
W. Rayment & Son, butcher
Art & Framing
The Leather Shop
Matthews, jewellers
National Westminster Bank
NEWNHAM STREET
Brands, florist, pets
Boots, chemist
Co-operative, groceries
Co-operative, Home & Wear
Thornhills, bakers
Castle Homes
Bendall Roberts, solicitor
Cutlacks, ironmongers
Stage Coach, restaurant
Ladbrokes, betting shop
Ely Floor & Tile Centre
The Pet Shop
Fleur, fashions
The Coffee Mill
Speed & Co, insurance brokers
Borland's Distinctive Shoes
City Cycle Centre, toys, DIY
G. & J. Peck, ironmongers
Lunch Box

1900, (1930 underlined)

(Not all 1930 businesses appear, only those trading in 1900 or 1990.)

centre block
Corn Exchange & Public Room

west side

J. Newstead, fishmonger
W.M. Kempton, fruiterer

north side

J. Barwick, provision merchant
White Hart (Mrs Egelton)
Tem'nce Hotel (J. Turner)
H. Leete, CC Surveyor
Club Inn (A.C. Allen)
Geo M. Hall, solicitor
Harold Archer, commissioner for oaths
(Vineyards, T.B. Granger)

east side

Coote & son, coal merchant
Hunt & Co, shoe repairer
J.W. Haylock, boots & shoes

south side

J. Houghton, draper
H. Copley, solicitor

BUTTERMARKET
G. Dove, tobacconist
J.F. Burrows, newsr
Fisher & Co, watchmaker & jeweller
P.F. Tow, fishmonger
Mrs Toombs, hairdresser
Toombs' eating house

BROAD STREET
west side from north

F. Cope, grocer
G.A. Toombs, hairdresser
E. Blanchflower, butcher
A.C. Lemon, butcher
M. & J. Porter, bakers
Jocobs' ale stores
Chas Williams, sweets
Mrs Bates, shopkeeper
Susan Middleditch, shop
James Harris, dyer
Coach & Horses (A.J. Buk)
W. Blake, furnisher
E. Lubbock, fancy shop
Geo Dobson, ham curer
H. Morgan, painter & shopkeeper
Sub-Post Office
Mrs Fox, jeweller
Temperance Hotel (W. Burchell)

1990, (1930 underlined)

Kemptons, greengrocer

Nationwide Anglia, building society
Kemptons

White Hart (closed)
Fish Bar & Café
Post Office
Echo & Co, fashions
V. Heath & Son, haberdashers
Tesco, Home & Wear

Archer House, solicitors

Cheffins, Grain & Comins, estate agents
Ely Weekly News
Wraggs Coffee Shop
Tandem, shoes

(City of Ely Hand Laundry & Nash & Co, now Cheffins Grain & Comins, 1930 Brunning's, tobacco, in Buttermarket – now D & F)
D & F Supplies

Fisher & Co, jewellers

Prudential Properties
United News Shops
G A Property Services
Washeteria
Granada TV
Eastern Electricity
Ladbrooke's betting shop
Midland Bank
Reflections

BROAD STREET
west side from north

N F U

Coffee & Cream
Dental Surgeon
Monica Sindall, photographer

1900, (1930 underlined(

(E.B. Claxton, Park Cottage)
H.T. Fear, grocer, tea dealer

George Porter, butcher

F.J. Aveling, painter & shopkeeper
C. Abbey, coachbuilder
J. Cross, baker
C. Brown, fishmonger
R. Green, fishmonger
J. Long, butcher

J. Graven, engineer
W. Turner, grocer

W. Buckle, carpenter & shopkeeper

east side from north

Glazier's Arms (Mrs Day)

W. Taylor, insurance agent
Bell & Theobald, timber merchant
Wheel Inn
Arthur Snell, gardener
SCHOOL
J.W. Howe, shopkeeper

W.P. Snell, nurseryman
John Hardy, fellmonger
Three Blackbirds (Geo Bruce)
Cutter Tap (Mrs Hill)
MILLERS SQUARE
Co-operative Stores
ST PETER'S CHURCH

STATION ROAD
south side from west

Black Swan (Mrs Berridge)
Gas Works & Showroom
John Negus, wheelwright
Harry Bickley, barber
T. Runciman, vet
Angel Hotel (Jas Speed)

north side from west

T.A. Guyatt, gas manager
G E Refreshment Room assist
W. Langhorne, painter

King Charles in the Oak
Railway Tavern
Miss Langhorn, shopkeeper
U. Cross & Sons, coal merchants
Crown Inn (J. Maltpress)
Richard Lupson, farmer
J. Hawkes & Son, coal merchants
Coote & Son, coal merchants

1990 (1930 underlined)

Neaves & Neat, employment agency
Surma Tandoori, Indian restaurant

1st Call Hire
Eagle Home Interiors Ltd

(1930 A. Wood & Co, woodyard now Jewson's, builders merchants
1900 Bell & Theob on west side
Denston, confectionery & photographs)

Ely Upholstery & Carpet Services Ltd
Tesco Stores

A T S Tyres
Hair by Gwendoline Jones
Images, fashions
Alan Fish Bar
Mirage Unisex Salon, hairdresser
Jewson, builders' merchants
Stapleton's Tyre & Exhaust
Jackson & Smith, vet
Graven's Car Hire Ltd
ST PETER'S CHURCH

Tuck Shop
Angel Inn
S & Y Haulage

St Peter's Garage
Trevor Benton Group, garage
Standen's, agricultural implement manufacturer
G H Builders & Developers
Dale Hire Ltd, care hire

Index

Figures in italics refer to illustrations

ENDPAPERS — FRONT: This c1700 version of the Jonas Moore map (originally produced 1654) gives information about Ely and the surrounding area: drainage channels, routes of roads or tracks, enclosures and particularly the course of the River Ouse near Ely. BACK: Surveyed 1885 and published 1886, this map shows how little the central street pattern has changed throughout the centuries. Beyond this section, to the north of Lynn Road, Butts Drove is shown and opposite, New Barns House (now part of the RAF Hospital Officers' Mess). The GER line cuts across Babylon through residents' gardens. (ULC)